THE ULTIMATE WEAPON

WEAPON

Terrorists and
World Order

The Ultimate Weapon

Terrorists and World Order

Jan Schreiber

WILLIAM MORROW AND COMPANY, INC.

NEW YORK   1978

FOR

DAMON

_____

Printed in the United States of America.

Library of Congress Cataloging in Publication Data

Schreiber, Jan Edward (date)
    The ultimate weapon.

    Includes bibliographical references and index.
    1. Terrorism. 2. Terrorists. 3. Hostages.
I. Title.
HV6431.S37   327   77-15534
ISBN 0-688-03277-X
ISBN 0-688-08277-7 pbk.

BOOK DESIGN   CARL WEISS

First Edition

1 2 3 4 5 6 7 8 9 10

PREFACE

WHAT STARTED AS A SIMPLE TASK BECAME A LONG AND EN-
grossing project. Shortly after I joined the staff of the Harvard
Center for Criminal Justice in January 1976, I was asked to
attend a conference on terrorism in Rochester, Michigan, and,
on the basis of the proceedings, as well as conversations with
the other participants and my own research, produce a small
monograph on the basic issues of terrorism. I did these things
(which were quite separate from my regular duties at Harvard), and in due course that work appeared as part of a
large volume published in a small way by the cosponsors of
the conference, the International Centre for Comparative
Criminology in Montreal. Long before the volume came out,
however, Denis Szabo, the director of the Montreal Centre,
suggested that I should write a full-size book on the subject.
I was receptive to the idea, since terrorism lies in an area of
considerable interest to me as a poet and social scientist: the
study of groups for whom violence is a socially cohesive element, a focus for the disparate energies of widely varying
personalities. I viewed terrorism as a potential case study, and
a life study, for a still larger and more ambitious work that
continues to form itself in my mind and is not yet ready to be
written.

Thanks to M. Szabo's suggestion I attended a second conference, this one on hijacking, held in Santa Margherita, Italy,
before I began the more solitary research for this book. To
the participants at both conferences, a few of whom appear
by name in these pages, I am indebted for many ideas (some
of them transmuted herein) and even for an occasional turn
of phrase. To Lloyd Ohlin, codirector of the Harvard Center
for Criminal Justice, I am grateful for some useful early discussions and for his cooperation in providing a flexible re-

search schedule at the Center while this book was being written.

Other useful conversations took place at Contract Research Corporation (my main center of activity) and at Wesleyan University, where my wife teaches and where I am a visiting diner. To the participants in all these discussions, who might well and justly repudiate their part in a book over which they had no control, I am duly grateful.

J.S.
August 1977

Contents

PREFACE

I / THE GOD FROM THE MACHINE 13

II / TERRORISTS AND VICTIMS, HEARTS AND MINDS 31

III / HARDENING THE TARGET 62

IV / FEAR AND TREMBLING: THE HOSTAGE GAME 94

V / THE GRAND STRATEGIES OF TERROR 126

VI / WHO WILL BELL THE CAT? 148

VII / THE TERRORIST IN CAPTIVITY 171

EPILOGUE 199

NOTES 208

INDEX 213

*If this land cannot be a home for everyone,
it cannot be a home for anyone.*

—URBANO

I

THE GOD
FROM THE MACHINE

"IF WE THROW BOMBS, IT IS NOT OUR RESPONSIBILITY. YOU may care for the death of a child, but the whole world ignored the death of Palestinian children for 22 years. We are not responsible." So, in 1970, Leila Khaled justified the actions of her fellow Arab terrorists and, by implication, of terrorists in all countries. In a world accustomed to placing more value on ends than means, the terrorist is the supreme pragmatist. No deed is too brazen or too grisly, so long as it gets the job done: the change of social structure or the sought-after revolution. Like anyone who deals in the politics of power, he lives in a climate of moral ambiguity. Renowned as a particularly heartless victimizer, he often sees himself, by contrast, as society's victim, someone driven to commit certain appalling acts by the blatant insensitivity of the world to the needs and aspirations of the people he represents. Carlos Marighella, the Brazilian urban guerrilla theorist, explained, "Kidnapping is used to exchange or liberate imprisoned revolutionary comrades, or to force suspension of torture in the jail cells of the military dictatorship. . . . The kidnapping of North American residents or visitors in Brazil constitutes a form of protest against the penetration and domination of United States imperialism in our country." But though terrorism is a response to someone else's aggression, the terrorist does not disclaim credit for the form of that response. "There is no other way for us," a member of the Japanese United Red Army maintains. "Violent actions, such as those we have used constantly in fighting the enemy, are shocking. We *want* to shock people, everywhere. . . . It is our only way of communicating with the people."

Noble or monstrous? Victim or murderer? Champion of

the disenfranchised or scourge of the innocent? As we first encounter him in the blurred images of videotapes, the patchy clandestine interviews, or the rhetoric of guerrilla handbooks, United Nations debates, and official denunciations, the terrorist seems an unreal figure: an evil force out of an old morality play or the bad guy in a B-movie. He makes a large claim on imagination but little on sympathy. He is feared and loathed if we are near his victims, quickly forgotten if we are not. No punishment, it seems, would be too great for him. But what is he in fact? What distinguishes terrorism from any wanton act of kidnapping or bomb throwing or mass murder? What are the differences between terrorism and guerrilla warfare, or any other kind of warfare, for that matter? What motivations, concerns, alliances, techniques, or grievances unite the Italian kidnapper with the Irish bomb thrower, the Lebanese assassin with the American urban guerrilla? We need, to begin with, a definition grounded not in theories but in persons and events.

A series of instances, chosen haphazardly around the unconsidered use of the word "terrorism," illustrates the range of behavior that definitions must comprehend.

In Uruguay members of the guerrilla organization called the Tupamaros kidnap two American officials and a Brazilian diplomat as part of a long campaign to topple the government and restructure the economy. They demand the release of political prisoners—previously captured members of their band —as a condition of the hostages' survival. The deadline passes, the government does not negotiate, and one of the Americans is shot. Weeks drag on; demands are modified; the guerrillas now insist that the government publish their 1,200-word political manifesto in return for release of the remaining hostages. Again, no cooperation. Eventually one hostage is set free when his wife privately arranges a ransom payment; the other, having suffered a heart attack, is deposited on a stretcher at the entrance to a hospital.

In the United States a bomb goes off in the middle of the night in the Army Mathematics Research Center at the University of Wisconsin, killing one researcher and completely destroying the building. Credit is claimed by the New Year's Gang, who say they regret the death but not the destruction, which they caused to protest the university's involvement in military research.

At Lod International Airport in Tel Aviv, the passengers have just landed on an Air France jet. They are milling about on the lower concourse, waiting for their luggage. The conveyor belt begins to move and after a while the bags appear, moving in slow succession as passengers reach out to claim them. Three Japanese passengers step forward and take two valises off the belt. The crowd is beginning to thicken. Suddenly the three pull grenades and Czech-made machine guns from their cases and with businesslike deliberation begin lobbing the grenades and raking the crowd with bullets. People scream and cower in terror. The terrorists slip in the blood and fall. One is accidentally shot by a companion, one is killed by his own grenade, and one is arrested. By the time the guns have stopped, twenty-four travelers lie dead; seventy-six others are wounded. Hours afterward, while the world is still numb with shock, Israel's political enemies step forward to claim credit for the act. The Popular Front for the Liberation of Palestine announces that the massacre is the work of one of its units, part of the extension of the Palestine struggle into the civilian heart of Israel, where everyone, national and foreigner, soldier and noncombatant, is seen as the enemy of the displaced Palestinian.

Weeks later, while flying over Turkey, a West German plane is hijacked by Arabs and used to secure the release of the guerrillas who staged a kidnapping at the 1972 Olympic games in which eleven Israeli athletes were killed.

Kidnap, bombing, shooting, airplane hijacking—besides death, destruction, and the associated terror, what do these acts have in common? Most notably they are acts perpetrated by groups, or by individuals as representatives of groups, who seek not to hide their responsibility but to advertise it. A gangland killing may be just as wanton and just as much a collective effort, but it is seldom boasted of in the public press; its motive or further purpose may be speculated on but is rarely announced. The gang's business is not to talk to the public but to settle internal scores. Similarly, the ordinary kidnapper may make use of the public media to demand ransom money, but he takes pains to conceal his identity. By contrast, acts of the kind just described seem staged— designed to capture attention and focus it on an identifiable group with a clearly enunciated cause. Very often the occasion of the crime is also an occasion for a statement, sometimes a demand, sometimes a threat. Spectacle, fear, excitement, and a message—such acts resemble a form of theater.

It is theater with a seemingly endless variety of resources. Property may be destroyed in the form of buildings, conveyances, or records. Lives may be taken or threatened. The threats—backed by periodic killings or torture—may be used to extort money, the release of prisoners, the publication of manifestos, or safe conduct to another country far from the scene of the crime. To the "traditional" old-style bombs, dynamite, or TNT that used to be planted in a building or beneath a street or lobbed from under an overcoat at a passing procession, our technology has added modern plastic bombs, letter bombs that can be mailed to the recipient-victim, automobile bombs that will destroy a car and its occupants as soon as the key is switched on, and the possibility, which equally fascinates and horrifies, of nuclear bombs available to private individuals, some of whom may have less of a sense of responsibility than governments have.

Certain modern weapons developed for military use may suit the needs of the terrorist as well. A single man or woman can operate portable missile launchers like the Russian Strela or the American Redeye, thus commanding an unprecedented range and destructive capacity. Even the strategic use of traditional weapons remains potent. Shootings may be selective— as when an ambassador or head of state is assassinated—or indiscriminate, as at the Lod Airport massacre. Individuals may be kidnapped and held for whatever concessions the terrorists are able to extort, or an entire planeload of people can be held hostage in a desperate ploy that threatens the hijacker's life along with the lives of his victims.

Through these diverse actions, the means by which terrorists of various persuasions announce themselves to the world, run other common threads. All such ploys are aimed at disturbing the state; by this means terrorists in effect declare war on the government they oppose. To listen to the announcements of bombers or kidnappers through the whine and crackle of high-strung rhetoric is to discover that a terrorist is a person with a radical social program, one not recognized by the government in power. ("Radical," of course, does not necessarily mean "progressive.") This explains why the terrorist has to use every means available to call public attention to his own organization as a preferable alternative. Such publicity can in fact be considered an integral part of terrorism. It follows that *unexplained* violence is by definition not terrorist violence. When in late 1975 a bomb went off in a luggage locker in New York's LaGuardia Airport, killing eleven people, news reporters were quick to ascribe the wanton destruction to terrorists. But this particular explosion could not have been the work or terrorists by the criterion we have provisionally established (though it may have been an unplanned detonation of a terrorist bomb intended for another purpose), because no terrorist organization claimed credit for the blast. Terrorism, according to this view, is a form of threat. With no one to take responsibility, there can be no effective threat, no warning that unless major concessions are made, the belligerent group will do something even worse next time.

Another almost universal characteristic is the element of surprise. No one is deceived that any terrorist group has the strength to disable an entire country. If it had, it would already be an independent nation defending itself against other terrorists and other nations. But in its very weakness lies its strategy: it substitutes for omnipotence the sudden strike at a vulnerable spot from an unexpected quarter. By attacking one of the millions of impossible-to-defend targets that every country offers if one ignores the rules of conventional warfare, the terrorist creates the illusion of ubiquity: his forces are in every alley; at any moment he may strike again.

If the terrorist act is theater, then, it is theater by surprise and in the interests of a political program. "Which is better for our cause?" asked the Algerian Front de Liberation Nationale: "to kill ten enemies in some gulch . . . or one in Algiers, which will be written up in the American press the next day? If we are going to risk our lives we must make our struggle known. We could kill hundreds of colonialist soldiers without ever making news." It is possible to diagram the process of terrorist communication by means of a triangle in which the terrorist is the subject, the opposing government is the object, and the victim is the medium.

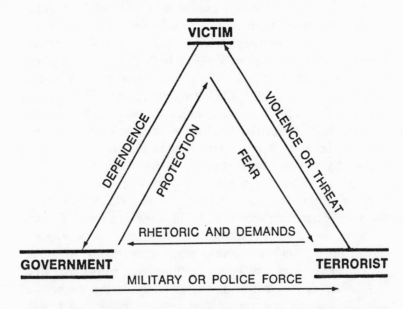

The messages are various: "Publish our demands," "Release our prisoners," "Stop consorting with our enemies"—but always, underlying them, runs one message that does not change: "Notice us, reckon with us, take our presence and our anger seriously." To the recipient government these requests are not pleas and supplications, they are the demands of one belligerent upon another. This is so because they are backed up by violence and the threat of violence, and chances are very good that at least some of those threats will be carried out.

The choice of victim, the third point in the triangle, is often random or incidental. He dies not because the group has anything against him personally but because his death (or the threat of it) will alarm many people and thereby demonstrate to society at large that his killers or kidnappers are deadly forces, however small their numbers. The resulting terror in the population at large compels the unwary government to overreact. To offer any significant level of protection in the face of widespread demands for security and a general demoralization produced by fear is to provide more protection than governments can afford or peacetime populations will long tolerate. But because so little is known about the shadowy army that may strike anywhere, only repressive measures on a rather large scale appear to offer any hope of stopping terrorist violence or rooting out terrorist enclaves. In extraordinary circumstances people will sometimes tolerate such government overreaction in hopes of being kept safe. Thus when the Canadian government invoked the War Measures Act in 1970 in response to a double political kidnapping, people were almost relieved. Even the socialist opposition, the New Democratic Party, accepted the strict measures, which among other things made warrantless searches and arrests legal, with such equanimity (leader Tommy Douglas merely grumbled that it was "using a sledgehammer to crack a peanut") that observers believed the party secretly welcomed them in the hope that they would stem a tide of separatist terrorism.

The terrorist's victims, then, are not the end of the crime but an intermediary. They are a means of gaining power and conveying a message to society at large. An Irish lawyer and sometime terrorist, Myles Shevlin, tried to explain this to journalist Gerald McKnight. "When the decision has to be taken, say, that Gerry McKnight is to be blown to pieces, this isn't easy. But it has to be done. Of course, it involves terrible strain on the individuals, but they'll stand up to it. They'll do what has to be done." Directed ultimately against the state, the terrorist act is a form of political behavior, even though it is behavior that the majority of people would reject.

From this overview of activities falling under the general

rubric of terrorism, it is possible to trace certain distinctive features that begin to cohere as a definition. Among the myriad causes of human violence, what the acts we are concerned with have in common is their political motive—usually in the form of a desire to overturn an established government. What the people who commit them have in common is some form of organization, however rudimentary. To oppose a government you need a potential government to put in its place—or at least a group of conspirators to undermine it effectively. The solitary assassin stalks about the fringes of terrorism: when he is genuinely alone his motives are usually not political but personal; when he enlists conspirators he must find a common grievance and a common goal—that is, he becomes "politicized." When his organization directs its energies against the state, it commits a political act. Finally, what the immediate victims of terrorism have in common is their noninvolvement: with the exception of diplomats, national leaders, and corporation executives they are not part of the terrorist's real target; they are simply a means to an end. In any case the chosen victim is usually not a soldier, since no war has been declared and the terrorist is not equipped to fight one.

Definitions are important, since the rhetoric of political denunciation brands with the term "terrorist" those people whom others may call "revolutionaries," "freedom fighters," or "founding fathers," and since, on the other side, small-time criminals or unhinged fanatics have dignified their images with pretended political motives. In what follows we will not go far wrong if we define terrorism as a political act, ordinarily committed by an organized group, involving death or the threat of death to noncombatants. This definition excludes private kidnappings designed to extort money, and it excludes both gangland killings prompted by revenge motives or power struggles and well-publicized but essentially nonpolitical acts of murder, even mass murder, committed by deranged individuals or fanatical groups. What makes the terrorist act political is its motive and its direction: it must be the intent of the perpetrators to harm or radically alter the state. Nor is motive in such cases as speculative as it often is in ordinary murder cases; we have already seen that terrorist acts are almost invariably accompanied by a public statement of purposes and demands.

Yet, though announced intentions sometimes make matters clear, across the broad spectrum of political expression it is hard to discern, in many specific cases, what is and is not truly political. Frequently, because news travels fast, a kind of "echo effect" can be observed: a series of terroristlike activities with progressively weaker political motives occurring over a span of a few months. In 1970 Uruguay's Tupamaros, the violently antigovernment terrorist group, kidnapped AID official Daniel Mitrione, accused him of helping to train special police forces in the use of torture techniques, and demanded as a condition of his safe return that their government release all political prisoners in Uruguay. Upon the Uruguayan government's refusal to negotiate, supported by American reluctance either to come to Mitrione's assistance or to exert pressure on Uruguay (a pressure that in countless other ways had become a fact of life in the South American country), the Tupamaros voted among themselves to shoot the official. The "execution" was carried out on August 9, 1970, and the following day police found Mitrione's body in the trunk of an abandoned car.

In 1971 Costa-Gavras made the film *State of Siege*, which offered a sympathetic fictionalized treatment of the Tupamaros and depicted Mitrione's kidnapping and death. The film played extensively in American theaters through 1973.

In May 1973, following more than a year of kidnapping of corporate executives, many of them heads of auto companies, by the Argentine terrorist group called ERP (whose initials stand for Ejército Revolucionario Popular, or People's Revolutionary Army), an unusual accommodation was reached. Some of the first victims of these kidnappings had been shot, as was Oberdan Sallustro, president of the Argentine branch of Italy's giant Fiat Motor Company, because of fatal hitches in the negotiations with the terrorists. But later kidnappings had resulted in the payment of millions of dollars in ransom to the revolutionaries, and the freeing of the victims. Now the Argentine office of the Ford Motor Company agreed, as a condition of protection from further kidnap attempts, that it would distribute a million dollars' worth of medical supplies, food, and educational materials to Argentina's poor. Four hundred thousand dollars were to be shared by two hospitals in Buenos Aires and Catamarca. Ford would supply ambulances for use in various provinces. The company began distributing $200,000 worth of dried milk in the slums surrounding Buenos Aires, and it committed $300,000 to supplies for needy schools in the city. Edgar R. Molina, Ford's vice-president for Asian, Pacific, and Latin American operations, said that the gesture was in response to a machine gun attack the day before on two Ford executives, followed by ERP's warning that there would be further such attacks if Ford did not provide a million dollars' worth of welfare supplies. Apparently justifying the response to the shareholders, Molina explained with obvious reluctance, "We have no choice but to meet the demands." Whatever else might be said of this terrorist ploy, it was an inspired piece of revolutionary theater.

Then, early in 1974, a tiny, loosely formed terrorist organization in California calling itself the Symbionese Liberation Army moved on from a program built on assassinating local officials with cyanide bullets and in a spectacular move kidnapped newspaper heiress Patricia Hearst. National attention was immediately focused on the event, which was given wide coverage in the media. The pattern of the SLA demands and their communication through Berkeley radio station KPFA corresponded in many details to the methods used by the kidnappers in Costa-Gavras' film. But the demands were notably different. Randolph Hearst, the victim's father, was to put up an amount ranging from $2 million to an impossible $600 million (the demands varied during the negotiations) to feed California's poor. The program was actually put into operation, and before long in the poor neighborhoods of Oakland lines were forming at the backs of trucks from which volunteers handed out bags of groceries. Abuses were rampant, and the program began to look like a more spectacular but shorter-lived version of the federal food stamp program. It was evident that the action had not been well thought out and that the improvised People in Need giveaway (as it was called) was an ultimately futile gesture, since it could have no lasting effect on the families it was designed to help. Beyond its objection to present social inequities the SLA had evolved no coherent social program.

Shortly after these events occurred, a rash of minor kidnappings broke out in various parts of the country. In Atlanta newspaper editor J. Reginald Murphy was kidnapped by a couple calling themselves members of the American Revolutionary Army. They issued a statement through Murphy calling for the resignation of all members of Congress and "free elections to return American government to the American people." However, their only demands in return for Murphy's release were for money. The money was paid, Murphy was set free, and his captors were apprehended not long afterward.

A few days later on Long Island, John Calzadilla, an eight-year-old boy, was abducted on his way home from school. His youthful captors returned him within a week, even though the ransom payment was intercepted. There was no attempt at all to make this kidnapping look like a political act.

Linked together by media publicity, then, are a series of kidnappings, each with less clearly defined political motivations than its predecessor. Thus actions shade off from plainly terrorist enterprises to loose confederations of dissidents, and from there to something else; but the exact points of demarcation will be disputed. Everyone agrees in calling the Tupamaros a terrorist group, and everyone would agree that the Calzadilla kidnappers were common criminals. But are the SLA terrorists? Probably. And the American Revolutionary Army? Probably not.

In addition, however, since the terrorist act not only opposes the policies or even the existence of the state but also violates its laws, it looks very much like a kind of political crime: that is, a crime subject to the punishment usually accorded to such acts, but committed for political reasons.

The line between common crime and political crime is not easy to draw. Officially there is no political crime in the United States; yet treason can hardly be called anything else, and those states that provide especially severe, usually capital, penalties for killing a police officer are also recognizing a political crime: to flout the authority of the state by killing its officers is inherently more serious than to kill an ordinary citizen. However, there are many terrorist acts which, as acts, have nothing to distinguish them from common crimes like murder, kidnapping, or air piracy. They are not political within any statutory definition, since such definitions are not based on a distinction between political and nonpolitical motives. From a legal point of view they remain common crimes, but they are nevertheless political acts, and what distinguishes them as such is motive.

Given its essentially political motive, the terrorist act may have various immediate purposes. It may be committed to gain personal freedom, to secure the release of imprisoned comrades, to bring about some specific action such as the cessation of military research, to call attention to grievances, or to take revenge against an enemy state or ethnic community. In the United States, attempts to gain personal freedom through terrorist acts used to take the form of skyjackings by Cuban exiles bent on returning to their homeland. Elsewhere terrorists have used skyjackings to secure the release of political prisoners belonging to their own organization or to related guerrilla groups. Skyjacking is of course only one of many ways of capturing and holding hostages. Hostage taking in itself has proved to be an effective way for a weak organization to extort concessions from a much more powerful government, including such concessions as the release of prisoners, the payment of ransom, the publication of demands, and the reform of prison conditions. Bombing may be used to disrupt normal activities, to call attention to the terrorist organization and its purposes, or, again, as an act of revenge. At times these purposes may be combined, and at times they may be diluted by the more personal motives of some of the participants. Some experts have pointed to the presence in certain terrorist organizations of violent or disturbed personalities who have tendencies to harm other people quite apart from ideology but use the stated purpose of the organization to justify their acts. Similarly, some professional criminals have been known to join terrorist organizations as a "cover" for their criminal activity.

But the presence of criminal or pathological elements in a terrorist organization does not change its essentially political character. Because of this character, both the causes and the potential solutions of the terrorist problem differ significantly from those associated with other types of violent crime. An act of terrorism can be thought of as the extension, or sometimes the first gambit, of a war declared by the terrorist organization against the state. In this unequal battle, the aims of the terrorists are to use what little strength they have to gain maximum leverage: If they could not hope to capture a city or a portion of the countryside, at least they can kidnap a diplomat and use his country's (and his family's) desires to protect him as a bargaining tool. If they cannot control or even perceptibly influence government policy toward war research, they can strike against the physical centers where such research takes place, and in the process they can destroy buildings, equipment, data, and sometimes personnel.

It's easy to see that the terrorist act is ordinarily committed by an organized group. As with any description of human phenomena, however, this one has imprecise edges. Does it make sense to talk about Hitler and Arafat in the same breath? Are oppression, cruelty, and mass murder as instruments of state policy essentially the same as unpredictable violence used as a weapon by the disenfranchised? If our purpose is only to pity the victims and deplore the attackers, then no further distinctions need be made. But attempts to control such violence, based on no further understanding than this, are bound to be simplistic and ineffectual. For further inquiry shows the purposes of the tyrant and of the true terrorist to be antithetical. The tyrant seeks to destroy dissent, the terrorist to arouse it. The tyrant therefore will publicize some of his own violence as a warning to the dissident, and be surreptitious about a great deal more; the terrorist calls attention to all his violent acts since they are testimony to the little power he has. Through his violence the tyrant speaks directly to those who might dare to challenge his authority; for the terrorist each violent act is a gesture toward the power structure he opposes, an attempt to communicate with the broader world, while the victims are secondary, mere instruments. The tyrant can be deposed, as the Greek colonels were, or he can die, as Franco did, and all at once a new order is possible. A terrorist can be shot, as Ché Guevara was, or a terrorist uprising put down, as in the case of Attica or the Mau Mau, and yet the conditions that give rise to the violence remain the same and the volcano may at any moment erupt again.

So it makes sense to separate out those terrorists who are not part of a government establishment: they are essentially different in their actions and motivations, and in society's response to them, from the dictators and strongmen whose methods they sometimes copy. But even having done this we face confusion. Both the act and its motive tend to shade off into other kinds of acts and other motives. The point at which a terrorist group becomes a genuine army, for example, cannot be defined exactly. Yet everyone knows that at some point Mao indubitably had an army, where earlier he had had only a band of followers; the outlawed Irish Republican Army is considered a terrorist group by its enemies, and it operates clandestinely, yet it has ranks and its own military discipline. If only an established government can have an army, then the army of every would-be government or government-in-exile is simply a guerrilla band, a terrorist organization. But suppose we argue that only an armed force that attacks civilian targets can be considered terrorist. In that case parts of almost every major modern army must be considered terrorist organizations as well, for they all have burned villages, raped women, shot children and old people, destroyed hospitals and places of worship. The terrorist lurks in more places than we like to think.

To define terrorism as a social phenomenon does little,

however, to settle a host of vexing legal questions caused by the unpreparedness of the world's legal codes to deal with this form of activity. Although the term has been with us since the French Revolution, it has come into currency only recently. Up until 1974, the *New York Times Index* had no listing under "Terrorism" but referred seekers to such sub-categories as "kidnapping" and "bombing." And even now no international agreement exists on the mere definition of terrorism, not to mention the appropriate response. Is it surprising, then, that international and national laws appear helpless in the face of much contemporary terrorist activity?

How should the terrorist be dealt with under international law? Is he a political criminal and therefore entitled to asylum by states such as West Germany that make it a point to be a haven for the persecuted and the politically prosecuted, or is he a common criminal and therefore subject to extradition? If he should be extradited, where to? Where can he get a fair trial for a deed attended by worldwide publicity? Or is his status that of a prisoner of war, to be interned and respected and someday to be repatriated if the nation he envisions ever comes to be born?

What is the effect of punishment on terrorists? Does a jail sentence deter, or is it an excuse for a further terrorist exploit designed to spring the imprisoned comrades? Should terrorists be executed, or would such a policy only intensify terrorist violence (might as well be hanged for a sheep as a lamb)? Can a terrorist be rehabilitated? And what is the meaning of "rehabilitation" in such a context?

Finally, how can we, the large, powerful, and complacent nations, protect ourselves against terrorist depredations? Should we invest in heightened security and enhanced police powers? Should we sacrifice some civil liberties, such as the right to move from place to place without notifying anyone, for the sake of better protection? Should we, as the Israelis have done, learn to be suspicious of large, unclaimed packages in public places?

It may be misleading to search for the root causes of terrorism. Psychologists predictably find some of them in human nature itself, and few thoughtful people would disagree, but human nature is also highly responsive to external conditions, among which are the society each person is compelled to live in. That society, in the midst of affluence and technological advance, may prove at times to be an effective molder of terrorists. It is a common observation that terrorism does not spring from a group so thoroughly subjugated that its members have lost both hope and self-respect. Iron-fisted regimes may have other problems, but threats from organized terrorist groups are usually not among them. But let that control begin to loosen, let a Franco falter or a Vorster seem insecure, and beneath the humdrum surface of daily life long-suppressed ideas and feelings begin to ferment and seethe. Just as the first advances toward full citizenship for black Americans in the 1950's signaled the advent of a Black Power movement with occasional propensities toward violence, so around the world Czech nationalists, Basque and French-Canadian separatists, Palestinian exiles, Irish home-rulers, African anti-colonialists, and South American guerrillas responded to the scent of independence and self-determination by arming themselves and making forays against the states that continued doing their best to contain them.

That they turned to arms rather than parliamentary process says as much about the societies they oppose as about themselves. Such societies are by no means uniformly inclined to dictatorship. Many in fact are pillars of Western democracy. But even democracy suffers from what may at times prove to be a fatal flaw: minorities do not make policy. In countries with a parliamentary system of government, minority groups may enter into coalitions that collectively can swing quite a lot of weight, but even here they often correctly perceive themselves to be effectively disenfranchised by the insensitive will of the majority—which, after all, provides for its own wants whenever it is forced to choose between conflicting interests. Ché Guevara premised that only when legal channels for social change have proved futile is the time ripe for guerrilla warfare. Conversely, when those channels begin to work for the minority, the guerrilla is deprived of some of his power base. Thus Canada, in many ways a model democracy, for years was prey to the terrorist depredations of the Quebec separatists, the FLQ. Only after René Lévesque was elected premier of Quebec on an avowed separatist platform did terrorist activity noticeably abate, and then for the very good reason that separatists believed they finally had access to the seat of power; it was no longer necessary to blow up buildings or kidnap officials in order to command attention.

Social and political mechanisms to cope with the aspirations and the anger that give rise to terrorist actions are extremely primitive, however, and usually depend much more on the coming to power of persuasive, charismatic leaders than on constitutional rules and legal procedures. And since most governments, like most institutions of any sort, resist change with a profound and steadfast inertia, the obvious approach of undercutting the potential terrorist by coopting his program is frequently the last one to be tried. Too many interests are arrayed against such a move, including the theoretically laudable interest in keeping a nation in one piece. Spain and Canada do not want to divide in two. Northern Ireland could not if she wanted to; the lives of Irish Catholics and Protestants are too much intertwined. Israel does not want to yield captured territory, inevitable though that is. Rhodesian and South African whites do not want to give up control of "their" countries.

And so they explore the lesser measures with all the ingenuity of the genuinely frightened. Buildings and prominent persons are carefully guarded. Nations publish bold statements about their refusal to negotiate with terrorists under any circumstances. Security checkpoints are installed in airports. Police painstakingly learn the techniques of hostage negotiation and how to help a motorcade bearing a dignitary avoid a terrorist ambush. Statesmen meet to draft international conventions for the prevention of political terrorism. International law enforcement agencies track the movements of known assassins, anarchists, and guerrillas. Prison officials try to figure out ways of making jails more secure. All the while, with cold-blooded persistence and cunning, harboring his grievance and mentally erecting his antigovernment barriers, the terrorist plots his moves as in an elaborate game of chess. Only the game is war—the primary basis for all competitive games—and the terrorist alone knows he is engaged in it even as he amasses his grenades. The next battle may be fought tomorrow, and in all probability the terrorist is the only one who knows of the battle in advance. He alone will choose the time and place, and he will make the first move. After that, things will begin to happen very fast.

II

TERRORISTS
AND VICTIMS,
HEARTS AND MINDS

"MORAL SUPERIORITY IS WHAT SUSTAINS THE URBAN GUER-rilla. Thanks to it, the urban guerrilla can accomplish his principal duty, which is to attack and survive. . . . It is not always possible to foresee everything, and the urban guerrilla cannot let himself become confused, or wait for orders. His duty is to act, to find adequate solutions for each problem he faces, and not to retreat. It is better to err acting than to do nothing for fear of erring. Without initiative there is no urban guerrilla warfare. Other important qualities in the urban guerrilla are the following: to be a good walker, to be able to stand up against fatigue, hunger, rain, heat. To know how to hide and to be vigilant. To conquer the art of dissembling. Never to fear danger. To behave the same way by day as by night. Not to act impetuously. To have unlimited patience. To remain calm and cool in the worst conditions and situations. Never to leave a track or trail. Not to get discouraged." In these sententious passages from his *Minimanual of the Urban Guerrilla,* written in the mid-sixties, the Brazilian revolutionary Carlos Marighella started to sketch the makeup of the ideal terrorist. While "terrorism" has a very restricted meaning in Marighella's terminology, the term applies to most activities of his urban guerrilla. Marighella concedes, "Terrorism is an arm the revolutionary can never relinquish. . . . It is an action the urban guerrilla must execute with the greatest cold bloodedness, calmness, and decision."

At first sight the portrait appears unrealistic, but that is not really the point. What matters is that other outnumbered and underequipped fighters in quite different circumstances have recognized the ascetic ideal that underlies the image. Fighting a jungle war rather than an urban one, Mau Mau insurgent Karari Njama wrote, "No one can serve two masters. In order to become a strong faithful warrior who would persevere to the last minute, one had to renounce all worldly wealth, including his family. . . . In fact, I had said goodbye to my wife. . . . I had warned her not to expect any sort of help from me for at least ten years' time. I had instructed her to take care of herself and our beloved daughter. I had trained myself to think of the fight, and the African Government; and nothing of the country's progress before independence. I had learned to forget all pleasures and imagination of the past. I confined my thoughts [to] the fight only—the end of which would open my thoughts to the normal world."

It is easy to see the religious overtones in such self-renouncing attitudes. And in fact the connections between religious devotion and murderous revolutionary zeal can be traced back for centuries. Early Crusaders, whose own sectarian loyalties were used to justify widespread murder and looting, returned from their eastern forays with wide-eyed accounts of a Muslim sect known as the Assassins. The name, derived from *hashishi,* apparently referred to a custom of performing violent exploits while high on cannabis. For the Assassins, who drew many of their beliefs from Islam, with its support of just rebellion and the murder of tyrants, killing under some circumstances, including the killing of Crusaders, amounted to a sacrament. They always used a dagger, and if discovery of this telltale weapon led to the apprehension of the killer, they appeared quite willing to suffer the death penalty for their act. "We are dealing," says Paul Wilkinson in his historical treatment of terrorism, "with the phenomenon of fanatical believers who killed because they believed that killing the unrighteous would guarantee their own salvation and assist in overthrowing a corrupt order." Far from being moral outcasts, then, these early terrorists considered themselves honorable and even good men.

So do their modern heirs. Marighella sums up: "Today to be an assailant or a terrorist is a quality that ennobles any honorable man because it is an act worthy of a revolutionary engaged in armed struggle against the shameful military dictatorship and its monstrosities." It is this element of moral conviction that differentiates terrorism in its psychological aspect from similar forms of violence and constitutes the basis for the paradigm that we explore in the following pages. Like any other person who is utterly convinced of the rightness of his cause—that is, like a devout religious convert—the terrorist is unshakable, often fanatical, inwardly assured. While his actions may resemble those of a common outlaw, his devotion exceeds that of all but the most patriotic soldiers. His assurance is his strength. It allows him to withstand the rigors of punishment, the temptation to make easy deals that might get him out of a tight spot, or the threat of death. With it he can negotiate with his opponents from a position of moral superiority, convinced that his cause is right while they are probably just carrying out orders and might in fact secretly sympathize with him. Indeed this conviction becomes a means of winning others over to the movement. Since his real enemy is ordinarily not his immediate victim but rather a hostile government or social system, it is often possible for the terrorist, paradoxically, to develop a rather close and friendly relationship with the person at whom he points his gun. Frequently, therefore, a terrorist group will speak regretfully of the necessity of using violence to achieve its ends, just as nations speak regretfully of the necessity of going to war over certain "just" causes.

Moral justification for violence is part of the modern rhetoric of world politics, whether articulated by nations who have the "right," in international law, to wage war, or by relatively obscure groups who arrogate such rights to themselves. Not infrequently, an entire terrorist exploit is given over to asserting, rather than acting on, these rights. Late in the summer of 1976, to take just one example, a group of Croatian exiles hijacked a TWA jet bound from New York to Chicago and forced it to fly to Paris by way of Montreal and London, dropping leaflets along its course to expound the group's cause. Calling themselves Fighters for a Free

Croatia, the hijackers contended that they represented three million exiles with "a moral right to demand a radical change in the American policies regarding occupied Croatia." They added, "We shall use as little violence as possible to achieve our demand." In fact they didn't use any—not directly at least. Although the hijackers appeared to passengers to be armed with awesome-looking plastic bombs, they were courteous and even solicitous as they went about their business aboard the plane. One of them stayed in the cockpit with the pilot and copilot, as they arranged the successive landing points of the short-range Boeing 727 jet, which can go only about 1,600 miles on a tank of fuel. The others walked up and down the rows of seats. At first some of the passengers were frightened by the very appearance of the hijackers. Said passenger Jim Perkins, "Two of the men showed us what we thought were explosive devices strapped to their persons. One of them was a real sinister-looking dude, with a heavy beard and dark glasses, and he was holding a device in his hands in front of him. The other was fingering a switch device and we could see wires going from the device into his clothing." But, he added, "they were so polite it was ridiculous." They told the passengers they were using the hijacking as a way of communicating their grievances to the world at large. The Croats were underrepresented in Yugoslavia's government, they said, and passengers who took the trouble to read the leaflets they circulated found a sober manifesto containing perhaps a one-sided view of historical events, but bearing no evidence of insanity or hysteria.

Some thirty hours later the episode was over. At Charles de Gaulle Airport in Paris police shot out the plane's tires, and negotiators gave the hijackers an ultimatum: Give up and be sent back to the U.S. or be seized, tried, and probably executed in France. After a hair-raising few hours when passengers feared they might be blown to bits, their captors surrendered. Their mission achieved, and facing the prospect of lighter sentences in America, the Croatians gave themselves up for extradition. Said one hijacker as he tore apart the cotton fluff in his fake bomb, "That's show biz!"

It would have been one of the cleverer terrorist actions of recent years, had it not been for a needless and irrelevant real bomb planted in Grand Central Terminal which killed a police officer. Threats were firm, precise, nonhysterical. Demands, including the publication of manifestos in major newspapers, could easily be met. In fact American papers seemed to welcome the chance to acquaint their readers with the anti-Tito Croatians. And passengers, struck by the terrorists' conviction, remarked that they had behaved like gentlemen and applauded them as they stepped off the plane. In short, a good show: Chicago-bound travelers, after recovering from their terrifying brush with Yugoslavia's political underworld, were treated to a glimpse of Paris, while the general public learned about another aggrieved minority. Only the needless bomb betrayed the cause.

Earlier we saw in the terrorist act a form of communication by means of a triangular relationship involving the terrorist, his immediate victim, and the authorities (usually an established government) whose actions he hopes ultimately to influence. It now appears that there is a fourth element in this diagram as well: the opinion of the general public, either in a particular country or in the world at large, which the terrorist group hopes to sway to its cause. Indeed, if the terrorist actions are to lead to genuine revolution, this element is the most important one, as George Prosser recognized in an article published in *Black Politics* while the Vietnam War was still in full flower: "It is essential that the people know that sabotage is being done, and why. Every act of sabotage, therefore, should be immediately followed by a communique from the underground headquarters, distributed by handbills, leaflets, underground press or radio, describing the act of sabotage and relating it to the struggle against the war, against imperialist intervention, against racism, and so forth. . . . The psychological impact of sabotage is so important that it can be said that any group which neglects it is throwing away half the battle." The precept applies not only to sabotage but to any other terrorist act; indeed, if the elements of perpetrator, victim, and authority are present, it is the act of communication with the general public that defines the proceedings as a terrorist maneuver. Terrorism is theater with a message.

Moral conviction that his cause is just and solicitous concern even for the ostensible victims of his act—these form an essential part of every careful terrorist's strategy. For the moment he may see himself in a lonely battle with almost all the rest of the world, but he does not want things to stay that way. Bearing in mind that we are separating out the politically motivated, largely selfless terrorist from the psychopath, the follower of kooky trends, and the small-time bandit, we can assert: *Every terrorist is an incipient revolutionary.* But although, as Mao said, power grows out of the barrel of a gun, it also grows when there is a solid base of social support, of people who can be brought to sympathize with the terrorists' cause. Recognizing this during the long war for Vietnamese independence, the Viet Cong in 1965 analyzed the events of their growing revolutionary movement and concluded in a self-critical vein: "With regard to the people, we have transgressed their free and democratic rights and have taken the lives of many persons who did not deserve a death sentence. . . . We have failed to apply the spirit of being firm in principles and flexible in practice. . . . We do not lean completely on the people and put confidence in the people. On the other hand, we are inclined to [coerce] the people and to lack sufficient determination to persuade the people, explain the Party's policy, and enable them to understand it clearly."

In truth such a policy is not easy to implement, but it can pay off handsomely when it works well. While the Mau Mau revolt in colonial Kenya was in full swing, the revolutionaries, normally confined to the forest areas, used to come out at night and enter the villages that were nominally under the control of the British colonial government. Karari Njama tells of one such occasion when some 240 people gathered in three huts on a farm near one of the villages. "[We] lectured to the villagers aiming at encouraging them and gaining their support and re-establishing communication links, bridge-system and a firm organization from the sub-location to the division. . . . After our long speeches we ate various types of food the women had brought to that home and our warriors carried bundles of raw food. One of the villagers took off his shoes and gave [them to] me. The sub-locational leader promised Ndiritu Thuita that he would send him all my requirements. It was already three in the morning when the meeting broke up." In such ways intermittently terrorized populations are made to feel that the revolution is not directed against them at all, that they in fact might easily join it; the real enemy is defined for them: it is the repressive government whose injustice they have only to recognize. The examples of this technique are drawn from full-blown revolutionary movements. They became revolutionary movements, however, because the technique worked. It is available to every terrorist.

Amid these public relations efforts, however, it is possible to lose sight of the truth that terrorism deals in the destruction of life and property. To see, with the suspension of disbelief, even death-dealing tactics as profoundly moral acts, however desperate, is to enter for a moment the world of the terrorist, who differs from the militarist in that he is self-appointed and thus responds to his own analysis of a social problem (and the attendant moral issues) rather than someone else's. Precisely because he is backed by such a minute consensus, however, he is readily and sometimes deeply affected by his relations with his victims, who as we have seen are also potential converts to his cause. This ambiguity of role, this simultaneous and conflicting impulse to kill and to convince, is fundamental to the psychology of the terrorist. That psychology becomes still more interesting when seen in interaction with the psychology of the victim, for it is an understatement to say that both are affected by their mutual contact.

Of the various available modes of action, terrorist bombing, of course, requires no direct contact with victims and thus allows the perpetrator mentally to inhabit, if he chooses, a world in which the lives of his enemies are of no more account than their property. Because of this the mode offers the smallest element of risk that the terrorist's sentiments may impair his pursuit of a rational strategy. With a curious ability to defend the humanity of one group while denying that of another, George Prosser wrote, "Bridges can be blasted, blocking waterways and impeding road or rail traffic. Water mains and pumping stations can be attacked, so that water pressure is reduced, preventing the suppression of fires. With still heavier weapons, such as mortars and machine guns, ammo depots and napalm storage dumps can be attacked. . . . Think of what it would mean to the longshoremen who load munitions into ships bound for Vietnam. . . . I say that it would make quite a difference if they were suddenly made to realize that theirs is a dangerous trade. The prospect of a Vietnamese mother or child being incinerated alive by napalm or white phosphorus may not touch them very deeply; but the prospect of their own precious hides being roasted would surely cause them to pause and reflect."

The psychology of bombing provides us with our first insight into a peculiar paradox of terrorist rationale: on the one hand the bomber claims the moral right to use violence on the unsuspecting; on the other hand he often denies direct responsibility, feels chance or his opponents to be responsible, and expresses regrets that innocent people have been hurt or killed. Here again it is possible to discern a parody of religious feeling and attitudes, wherein persons convinced of their own righteousness nevertheless believe they act at the direction of a higher power. It is easy, then, for the terrorist to construe the major problems of bombing as technical ones: a bomb cannot be readily directed toward a specific target; often it must be left somewhere with a timer set in the hope that the movements of the intended victim will bring him in range at the proper moment. Such uncertainty adds, if anything, to the emotional distance between the terrorist and his victim; not only need the bomber not see his target, he can act without knowing for sure that he is committing a murder. Then whether the victim ultimately lives or dies, the terrorist convinces himself that fate was the decisive accomplice.

Confronted, on occasion, with the necessity of observing

his deed in all its gory reality, even a seasoned terrorist may find his nerve failing him. "I was with a very hard man once," recalled IRA leader Ruairi O'Bradaigh. "We'd set up a mine together, to go off under a party of British soldiers. All we had to do was wait for them to position themselves, which shortly they did. Sure enough, they were right on target. And what did this hard fellow do? Just before making the connection, to explode the mine and blow them all to smithereens, he closed his eyes. Then he crossed himself and whispered devoutly: 'May the Lord, now, have mercy on their souls!' "

On the victim's side, the same element of arbitrary and sometimes capricious fate can enhance the effect of the terror. A mailbox that explodes and blinds the postman who was opening it, a letter bomb directed to an ambassador that blows up in the face of a deputy, killing him at once, a crudely made time bomb fashioned from a pressure cooker that kills a bomb squad officer moments after tests had indicated it was a dud, a university building that explodes in the middle of the night, killing the one researcher dedicated enough to be working there at four A.M.—such episodes appear the more horrifying because they are random: they might just as well have happened to someone else, or not have happened at all. A sufficient number of such explosions make the terrorist group seem ubiquitous, their purposes and methods supported by fate, chance, or—if your superstitions run in that direction—the gods of war.

Terrorists who substitute guns for bombs move a step closer to the victim. Some contact with the victim cannot be avoided in a shooting, even one that takes place outside the context of kidnapping. For Carlos Marighella, therefore, "Execution is a secret action in which the least possible number of urban guerrillas are involved. In many cases, the execution can be carried out by one sniper, patiently, alone and unknown, and operating in absolute secrecy and in cold blood." The reason, apart from security, is that groups have too many second thoughts; they reinforce each other's doubts. Of the two general target populations—unknown members of the general public and particular individuals who for the terrorists represent the hostile government authority—the latter are much preferred in most cases since terrorists believe their loss is a greater setback to the "enemy" while at the same time, being more credibly tied to the terrorists' political purpose, such an assassination is much easier to sell to the public at large. On the other hand, if all members of a nation are regarded by the terrorists as enemies—as Israelis and Palestinians tend to regard each other, or Catholics and Protestants in polarized Northern Ireland—they can be dehumanized in the minds of the terrorists' constituency, much as enemy populations during wartime, civilians as well as combatants, are dehumanized by propaganda. Under such circumstances the political disadvantages of essentially random murder sometimes weigh less in the minds of the guerrilla strategists than the psychological advantage gained by terrifying the opposing nation with unpredictable violence, creating the illusion that the terrorists' forces are larger than they are, and thus demoralizing a militarily superior enemy.

The corollary is that as the terrorist group comes to depend more heavily on world opinion and the support of certain nations in its struggle with a particular regime, it is likely to modify its tactics by deemphasizing the unpopular random murder of civilians. Evidence is plentiful in the history of the Arab-Israeli conflict. During 1974 Arab guerrillas representing such groups as the Popular Front for the Liberation of Palestine and the Popular Democratic Front for the Liberation of Palestine had made a number of raids into Israel from Lebanese soil, killing civilians in Kiryat Shmona, Ma'alot, Shamir, Nahariya, and other towns. (Israeli terror attacks against both military and civilian targets in Lebanon continued during the same period, accompanied by careful propaganda to make it clear to other nations that such raids were retaliatory and, despite their obvious effects, were not intended to kill civilians.) By midsummer the Palestine Liberation Organization, the umbrella body for the political and military guerrilla groups, announced that its forces would no longer use Lebanese bases for attacks against Israel. In early August the PLO opened an office in Moscow, and in September it joined in moves sponsored by the United States for a political settlement of the Arab-Israeli conflict. At this point the Popular Front, objecting to the compromise solution that would have resettled the Palestinians in the West Bank and the Gaza Strip, withdrew from the PLO and vowed to continue its guerrilla operations. Clearly, however, by accepting potential political solutions and the help of the great powers in arriving at them, the PLO had committed itself to changing its image from that of unprincipled cutthroat to patriotic freedom fighter and peace negotiator.

As we move along the continuum from minimal confrontation between terrorist and victim (in the case of bombing) toward increasing contact, we learn about that part of the terrorist's psychological makeup over which he has a large degree of control. But when we come to hostage taking, the terrorist episode suddenly takes on the character of a dynamic psychosocial process. To begin with, hostage taking happens over a significant period of time—long enough for the terrorist to experience certain influences on his initial resolve and his carefully achieved state of mind. Second, during this time the victim continuously (and the negotiator intermittently) confronts the terrorist, responds to him, and thereby affects his subsequent actions and feelings. Third, the victim himself is affected by the experience, often in ways he could never have predicted. Finally, the complex of response and counter-response between the hostage taker and his captives suggests a strategy to be pursued by negotiators who hope to avoid a violent outcome. For these reasons we shall find that our pursuit of the peculiar mystique of terrorism leads us at this point to explore the vagaries of hostage taking at considerably greater length than any other form of the art.

Members of the public, following newspaper or television reports of an airplane hijacking or the kidnapping of a diplomat, ordinarily identify with the victims. They do so for the very good reason that reporters concentrate on the victim's point of view. It is political orthodoxy to do so, since if we pity and sympathize with the victim while fearing and hating the terrorist, we can be led to think the terrorist is a bad person and his cause an evil cause: Surely one of *us* would never do such a thing. Besides, such media identification with the victim sells papers. "Will they escape," we wonder, and we talk over coffee about the pregnant woman or the family with three children trapped aboard the commandeered airplane.

There's no denying that it is a harrowing experience for the hostage; we would sympathize and feel anxious even without the prompting of news reporters. But in a different way it is also a harrowing experience for the hostage taker. Having made his move and announced his intentions to the authorities, he is bound to stand by the outcome of his action, and the outcome could easily be his death. Particularly in the case of an airplane hijacking his options are severely limited. If he is challenged by the crew while the plane is in flight his final recourse is the suicidal one of destroying the plane and all inside it. When the plane finally lands it will in all likelihood be surrounded by the forces of authorities hostile to him and his purpose. He may have succeeded in communicating his grievances to the world at large, but his own life is still very much at risk. If there is a forcible rescue attempt, some hostages may be killed, but some or all of the hijackers are sure to die. Every hijack attempt is therefore a serious flirtation with death. And in spite of his almost religious dedication to his cause, his willingness to die for it if necessary, the hijacker is uneasy staring death in the face for hours and even days on end. In the course of an exploit he is in the state of heightened emotional responsiveness, sometimes edging perilously close to hysteria.

In this state, which he shares with his captives, who fear death almost constantly and have virtually no control over events, he is susceptible to emotional involvement. As time passes he comes to feel a strong bond with his captives, and they with him. Both see themselves as a small enclave facing a hostile world. The results of this perception can work both for and against the terrorist. They work for him when his captives support him against the police or others who are trying to apprehend him. They work against him when his feeling for his captives betrays him into making an error of judgment.

As a result of a hostage-taking incident in Sweden in 1973 we have come to know this phenomenon as the "Stockholm syndrome." The Swedish episode was not a terrorist exploit but a bank robbery and escape attempt, yet it used essentially the same techniques we have come to associate with terrorism, and provoked many of the same psychological reactions. Early on the morning of August 23, 1973, Jan-Erik Olsson, a professional thief and safecracker recently escaped from prison, entered the Sveriges Kreditbank in Stockholm, produced a submachine gun he had been carrying under his coat, and began a bizarre adventure that involved four hostages and lasted six days. As one of the bank employees, at Olsson's loud, gun-enforced direction, was tying up his colleague, Kristin Ehnmark, she was incredulous. "I believed I was seeing something that could happen only in America." (This illusion may have been helped by Olsson's ploy of speaking English with an American accent.) Eventually isolated on the first floor of the bank with three women hostages and a man. Olsson demanded to police over the telephone that a fellow convict, Clark Olofsson, be sent to help him in the escape and that he be allowed to drive away from the bank with his hostages in tow. "I had lives for assets," Olsson later told writer Daniel Lang. "What could be more valuable?"

At that point Swedish Minister of Justice Lennart Geijer and Prime Minister Olof Palme were brought into the picture. After conferring hastily they decided that, though the police could offer various concessions as their judgment dictated, Olsson and his accomplice must not be allowed to leave the bank with the hostages. During the war of attrition conducted by the police over the following six days, hostage Kristin Ehnmark had a lengthy phone conversation with Prime Minister Palme in which she entreated him, unsuccessfully, to allow Olsson to carry out his plan of escape with his captives. The other hostages, too, soon found themselves feeling far more loyal and trusting toward the bank robbers than they felt toward the police or the government. Hostage Birgitta Lundblad recalled later that she had shunned contact with police negotiators. "I turned away from the police. I was part of a group—there didn't seem to be anything I could do about it." During a chilly night in the bank vault, Olsson put his gray coat around the third woman hostage, Elisabeth Oldgren. "Jan was a mixture of brutality and tenderness," she recalled wistfully. "I had known him only a day when I felt his coat around me, but I was sure he had been that way all his life."

Later, on another night, Olsson lay beside one of the female hostages. "May I caress you?" he asked. She told him he could. He did so, touching her breasts and hips and becoming increasingly aroused—but, she later said, she gently stopped him short of having sex with her. It wouldn't have worked; there wasn't time, it was too public, and, she added, by yielding she might have put herself too much in his power. She felt she needed to maintain some small edge of control.

Not only the women were susceptible. The sole male hostage, Sven Safstrom, remembered with confused incredulity that he had felt grateful when at one point Olsson said he planned to shoot him to show the police he meant business, but would only hit him in the leg. By contrast, when the hostages had contact with police negotiators, they appeared hostile, sullen, and distrustful.

Eventually the police succeeded in barricading the group— robbers and hostages—inside the vault and overcoming them with tear gas. Even after Olsson and his accomplice had surrendered their weapons the hostages remained loyal to them, refusing to emerge from the vault before the robbers, lest the police rush inside and shoot them. This feeling of loyalty and affection, of human bonds, was reciprocated. Months later Olsson recalled that the police themselves had pointed out that had he killed just one hostage, he would have called the police bluff and been allowed to flee the bank in his getaway car with the remaining captives. "I know that," Olsson had responded.

Analyzing the case after the fact, psychiatrist Lennart Ljungberg remarked, "As it happened, each of [the hostages] very much wanted to go on living. The same may have been true of the bank robbers." He was not so sure the same would have been true of political terrorists, with their devotion to ideology even in the face of death, but terrorists too prefer life, and most are convinced they can be more effective alive than as martyrs. "I don't care if I live or die!" yelled Zvonko Busic, the Croatian hijacker of the TWA jet, in a last desperate attempt to outbluff the authorities in Paris who had disabled his plane, but he did so knowing that the most explosive thing aboard the jet was his own pain, rage, and frustration. It's not wise to count on it, but terrorists will often compromise ideal strategy for quite human reasons.

As Daniel Lang reported in *The New Yorker*, after the Stockholm incident was over the hostages "persisted in thinking of the police as 'the enemy,' preferring to believe that it was the criminals to whom they owed their lives." In a sense, of course, they did. Hostages and hostage takers had brought each other through the adventure safely and with no small sacrifice.

This discovery is made anew by every hostage. It had been made in Canada three years earlier with sharp psychological acumen. In the summer of 1970, Lorraine Berzins, an officer with the Canadian Penitentiary Service, was taken hostage at knifepoint by an inmate of Warkworth Institution, where she was working. For the next eight hours he held her captive. "I had to develop a trust with him if I was going to save my life," she said. "For him to see me as an enemy was a danger to my survival. For him to start to trust me meant he would be less able to kill me." A scrupulous observer, she quickly perceived that her captor was "very, very frightened. . . . I started to try to reassure him, and I slowly discovered that he was more frightened than I was." With this awareness she also discovered a certain ambiguity. Her sympathies lay with her captor, yet she recognized that his behavior was essentially antisocial. "It didn't for one second mean that I approved of what he was doing, or that I sympathized with him as having a legitimate grievance. It was always very clear to me that what he was doing was endangering me and it was endangering him. Yet, in spite of that reality, I cared about his life."

She cared, of course, about her own as well. Had she not been trained as a corrections official she might have been more susceptible to the kidnapper's point of view—just as, four years later, Patricia Hearst would find herself won over to the cause of the earnest and forceful ideologues who abducted her.

Whether or not the captive becomes a convert, he is likely to be quite helpful to the hostage taker during negotiations with outside authorities. His life, after all, is at stake, and he recognizes that those on the outside can have little understanding of his real plight. They may be concerned for his safety, but they also have a number of other concerns that are inimical to the hostage: they have no real desire to yield to the terrorist's demands, to release political prisoners or give safe conduct; they do not want to lose face; they would like to set an example to other terrorists that hostage taking will not work. In short, they are engaged in a calculation: how little can they give up and still bring about the desired outcome? For the authorities the desired outcome is the capture of the kidnappers and the recovery of persons and property. Having been on the outside and indulged in some of those same calculations himself as he followed other kidnap episodes in the news, the hostage is deeply distrustful of the negotiators. Suppose they overreact? Suppose they decide to make an example of these terrorists and bring them down in a hail of bullets? "I had this very strong feeling that my life wasn't as important to the negotiators as it was to me," says Berzins. Yes, surely if it wants, the government can win in this unequal battle with the kidnappers, but quite possibly at the cost of a citizen—the hostage—who has made no bargain to give up his life for such a cause.

The point is so well understood by bank managers that officials charged with security in some banks have virtually given up trying to insist that a manager whose wife is kidnapped at home and held at gunpoint should report the deed before opening the till to get the ransom money. Managers simply don't trust police and bank executives to negotiate effectively for their wives' safety. David Godfrey of the Bank of Montreal tells of one manager whose wife was held for ransom and who took it on himself to negotiate the sum. He managed to reduce it to less than half the amount originally asked. His wife never forgave him.

And then there are even subtler psychological dynamics. The kidnapper is nervous in his dealings with authorities. He doesn't control them, he only has some leverage which may or may not be effective against them. The hostage, on the other hand, "belongs" to him. No question. One false move and there's a bullet through the brain or a knife across the throat. This state of affairs is gratifying to the kidnapper and puts him (relatively) at his ease. "She would of been a good woman," says the Misfit in a story by Flannery O'Connor, after terrorizing and ultimately shooting an old lady, "if it had been somebody there to shoot her every minute of her life." Many saner terrorists, who have no particular desire to kill their victims, fully agree. As a result, in the little world of the kidnapper and his captive, there is order, structure, and predictability. With the intrusion of the outside world, via the negotiators or the police, comes the contingent, the unforeseen, the possibly disruptive and destructive. Lorraine Berzins recalled, "There were moments when we established an equilibrium and I believed that things would work out. Whenever outside influences interfered with that equilibrium it all had to be redone."

Some negotiators have been slow to understand these dynamics and have jumped to the conclusion that the victim is selling out to his captors. In this way they have turned their backs on a potentially valuable ally. "Don't start to treat the hostage as an enemy," warns Berzins, "because that just makes the situation more difficult to resolve. If negotiators force hostages to take sides, they're going to side with the hostage-taker for survival reasons." Speaking of the hostage, she adds, "If your way of coping with anxiety is to project blame onto other people, you're obviously not going to project it onto the hostage-taker because that's too dangerous. You have a big stake in that relationship. The easiest target is the outside authorities."

America's most notorious example of this phenomenon was,

of course, Patty Hearst, whose about-face under the influence of the Symbionese Liberation Army seemed to have dumbfounded the general public, her parents, and even her defense attorneys. In truth it was entirely natural. She was a young woman from a sheltered background, with no particular ideas and no particular purpose. She was forcibly taken out of a privileged but directionless world and placed in another which was circumscribed, motivated, goal oriented, and filled with sanctions to punish undesirable behavior and reward its opposite. To an even greater extent than the Swedish bank hostages she was at the mercy of her captors, since no one but they knew where she was. Against their redefinition of good and evil, what did she have to offer?

Faced with an extreme act, people tend to take sides, to convince themselves that all virtue lies on one side and all wickedness on the other. In such a situation, acknowledging nuances or giving credit to an opponent for a plausible point of view is beyond the capacity of most hostages and most negotiators. At bottom we are psychological primitives and find it hard to see generous and selfish motives, or kind and cruel actions, in the same person. Generalizing from her own experience, Berzins observes, "There may be a clash between our different perceptions of a person's 'good' qualities alongside his criminal behavior. . . . If a person is not trained or experienced enough to be able to accommodate the seeming contradiction of the two, he may need to deny one in order to preserve the other. The hostage, to preserve the trust that his survival depends on, may need to see his captor as 'all good' to resolve the dissonance and maintain harmony between them. The outside authorities may be facing a similar dilemma: they may need to see the hostage-taker as 'all bad' in order to justify the drastic action they feel like taking."

So the relationship he develops with the hostage may do the kidnapper a lot of good, particularly to the extent that the hostage can persuade authorities to go slowly, not to force a crisis, to listen to the kidnapper's reasonable demands. Like any relationship of trust, however, it is also a potentially dangerous one that can backfire on the kidnapper. Jan-Erik Olsson learned this when he found it impossible, after several days with his hostages, to kill any one of them, even though in doing so he would have convinced the authorities he meant business and in that way could doubtless have won the concessions he demanded. For the hostage-taking ploy to succeed, the authorities must be persuaded that the terrorist *will kill the hostage if his demands are not met.* As soon as it becomes clear that this is unlikely to happen, the kidnapper has lost his case. He might as well surrender.

It is hardly necessary to add that even though the kidnapper may lose his margin of control by coming to like his hostages too much, such a development can only benefit the hostages. Perceiving this early in the episode, hostages usually have little trouble in forming bonds with their captors. These bonds may have saved many lives in the Entebbe hijacking in July 1976. During the long stay of the Air France passengers in the airport lounge in Uganda the hijackers had herded the Israeli nationals (as well as some non-Israeli Jews) into separate quarters. It was the most terrifying moment in the ordeal. At that point one of the hostages, Yitzhak David, approached the German man and woman who, guns at the ready, were directing them into the adjoining room. "Do you see this number on my arm?" asked Mr. David. "I got it in a German concentration camp. My parents were killed there. We thought that a new generation grew up in Germany. But today when I see you and your girl friend, it is difficult for us to believe that the Nazi movement died." The German, whose name was Böse, appeared to be taken aback. Haltingly, he tried to explain that he was a member of the Baader-Meinhof group— not a Nazi organization but a violent opponent of capitalism. He seemed at a loss to explain the connection between this ideology and the political purposes of the Arab terrorists who were directing the operation. Apparently, however, Mr. David's challenge roused both guilt and pity. For when the terrible moment of the rescue came and machine gun fire from the Israeli commando units tore through the night air, cutting down the hijackers standing guard outside the terminal, Böse suddenly appeared, gun in hand, in the passenger lounge, surveying the startled hostages stretched out on mattresses before him. He had only moments to live and he knew it. He could have killed most of the people in front of him with a flourish of his weapon. He stared distractedly at them and they at him. Then—"Retreat! Get down!" he shouted, both commands unnecessary and impossible to obey. Turning his gun on the advancing Israeli troops, he stood his ground and died in a wave of their bullets.

Later one of the Israeli hostages was still incredulous. "I couldn't believe my eyes when I realized he wasn't going to shoot us. I'm convinced it was the conversation he had with Yitzhak David about the death camps in Germany that made him spare us."

So far we have looked at critical moments in the course of a hostage-taking episode and have seen how the configuration of relationships at such moments affects the outcome of the episode for the kidnappers, the hostages, and the authorities involved. These moments unite to form a pattern, according to Wolfgang Salewski, a Munich psychologist. Commissioned by Lufthansa, the German airline, Salewski interviewed passengers and crew members who had been involved in a number of incidents. His report, *Luftpiraterie* (*Air Piracy*), was the basis for a training film made by Lufthansa to show crew members how to cope with actual hijack situations. What is most interesting in Salewski's conclusions for our purposes is his depiction of the curve of emotion that is perceptible on a hijacked airplane over the course of the episode. It is an oscillating curve, rising and falling between the extremes of desperation and euphoria and tending, with the protraction of the episode, to retreat from both extremes. If we follow the complete course of an airplane hijacking, based on several actual, documented occurrences, we will see these feelings develop out of events and hear the self-assessing comments of Salewski's interviewees at critical points in what was for each of them a harrowing adventure.

† †

It was a small jet, with perhaps forty passengers on board. Mostly businessmen, some couples traveling together, a few young people who appeared to be students. Frankfurt to Athens; for some of the passengers the second leg of a journey that had begun in New York. The stewardesses were going through their little pantomime with the oxygen masks while the public address system crackled in three languages as the plane taxied to the end of the runway. After a smooth takeoff the captain's voice came over the speaker announcing altitude and flying time and observing that he had turned off the "no smoking" signs. Near the front of the economy cabin a young man in a business suit closed a magazine in his lap to reveal a round object nestled between his legs. He picked it up and drew out a pin from it, then, in a continuation of the motion, reached into his jacket pocket. In the next moment he stood up, a pistol in his right hand, a grenade in his left. There were beads of sweat on his forehead. So far no one had noticed him.

He walked quickly to the kitchenette, followed by a tousle-haired young man in a nondescript yellow jacket. One of the stewardesses was taking plastic coffee cups from a compartment. She looked up and started to ask what she could do for them. Then her jaw dropped and she froze. They rushed at her, and the tousle-haired young man grabbed her from behind, jabbing a pistol under her chin. Needlessly, for she made no resistance and there were other crew members to worry about, the man in the business suit poked his gun inches before her eyes and brandished the grenade. "Keep quiet and nobody gets hurt," he gasped. "We're taking this plane." He was visibly shaking.

The man in the jacket half pushed her, half carried her, through the first-class section toward the cockpit. "Sit still and nobody gets hurt," shouted the man with the grenade. Almost with one motion the passengers selfconsciously placed their hands where they could be seen—on laps or seat rests. There were involuntary murmurs in one or two throats. "Shut up! Not a sound! Don't move!" The gun waved wildly over the faces as the man in the suit backed down the aisle, fol-

lowing his partner and the stewardess toward the cockpit.

"Open it!" whispered the tousle-haired man, pointing to the door. It was the first word he had spoken, and it sounded as if it were he, not the stewardess, who was held with an arm clenched around the throat. She opened it and his partner lurched inside, his pistol colliding with the back of the pilot's head. "Shut up! Don't move! Keep flying the plane! You do everything I say from now on." The pilot swallowed visibly, but otherwise he did not move, and he kept flying the plane.

"I sensed the hijackers were extremely nervous. If anybody had made a false move he would have been shot—I'm positive of that."

The hijackers wanted to go to Algeria. During the first hour after they made their move the one in the yellow jacket remained continuously in the cockpit, his arm locked around the stewardess's neck, his gun at her temple. She could feel the tension in his body, and everyone in the cockpit noticed his hoarse voice, his jittery motions as he ordered the captain to make the proper adjustments and radio the control tower at the airport in Algiers. "No funny business—no secret codes —no tricks. If somebody tries to pull a fast one the whole plane blows up, understand?"

The captain found he had to clear his throat several times before he could speak properly. "Yeah," he said. "Look, we get your message. We want this plane to land safely as much as you do. We gain nothing by not cooperating. We're all in the same boat."

In the back of the plane, meanwhile, another man in a business suit had stood up with a gun. He motioned to his partner that he had the rear of the plane covered. He stayed right at the back, near the rear lavatory, and played his pistol nervously over the silent passengers. "Come here!" his partner said to a second stewardess. She did so, and he jabbed his gun at her rib cage. "You stay right here," he told her. To the passengers: "Just stay in your seats and you won't get hurt."

Inside the cockpit the pilot was saying, "I don't know if we'll be able to land in Algiers. There's some doubt about the weather conditions."

"Shit!" said the hijacker. "I thought I just told you, no games. You're a dead man if you keep that up." He poked the pilot's neck with his revolver hard enough to hurt him. "Fly the goddamn plane the way I tell you."

"Right," said the pilot. "I just want to land her safely."

"Then shut up and concentrate," said the hijacker, and he pointed his gun back at the stewardess.

"Everything went so fast we didn't have time to think about it. We did what they told us; we sat still, kept our mouths shut, and waited to see what would happen next."

Curiously, the feeling of the crew toward the hijackers as time went on was not one of hatred, or even terror, but an odd kind of sympathy. It began to dawn on the stewardesses that their captors were as frightened as they were, that they had as much to lose if the adventure ended in catastrophe. The woman gripped by the man in the business suit noticed beads of sweat standing out on his forehead, though the cabin was not overly warm. She realized it came from excitement and almost unbearable anxiety. The psychic strain on him was greater than on her, for he had taken on the responsibility for the conduct of every man, woman, and child aboard the craft, and he had never done a thing like this before. A little incredulously she found herself feeling maternal toward him.

A short time later she noticed that his hold about her neck had relaxed somewhat. She ventured to look directly at him, taking care to move slowly. "Would you like a glass of water?" she asked.

"Yeah," he said, realizing just then how dry his throat was. He let her go. She moved to the tap while he covered her, watching her intently to make sure she was not trying to drug him. But she simply filled a paper cup and handed it to him. "Thanks," he said.

As the minutes passed a few voices could be heard among

the passengers in subdued conversation, almost as if the stewardess's gesture had been a signal for a return to something like normality. In the first-class section, the man in the yellow jacket briefly appeared outside the door of the cockpit. He had left his stewardess-hostage inside and his gun was down as he surveyed the passengers. Several of them glanced at him hopefully, as if to ask whether everything was all right. It came to him suddenly that to these people he was like a god, for he held their fate in his hands. The idea was tremendously appealing to him, and he felt a sudden urge to laugh rising in his throat. Hurriedly he turned and ducked back into the cockpit.

"We're right on course," the pilot told him. "Should be over Algiers in about 90 minutes." His hands were shaking.

"Steady does it," said the hijacker.

The man in the business suit was looking with some perplexity at the stewardess who had given him water. Finally he spoke.

"Look—every cop in Europe is after us after those Munich bombings. If they catch us and lock us up, how does that help the movement?" Then, inconsequentially, "This is a guerrilla war for the people."

"Yeah," responded the stewardess, surprised to find how wholeheartedly she agreed with him just then. "My cousin used to talk like that. He'd been in the navy and he hated it. Mainly for political reasons, of course, but also partly I think because he used to get seasick." She giggled.

"Oh yeah? Me too. God, I hate boats. Never get sick on airplanes, but boats—you can have 'em."

"You had to build up this really funny relationship. I mean, you know you're dependent on these guys for life or death, and yet you're trying to be buddies with them."

In the economy section the normal hum of conversation could be heard above the engines. A few passengers began reading books and magazines, though without really concentrating. A woman asked a hijacker's permission to use the lavatory and was allowed to do so. Still loosely holding his gun, the hijacker at the rear of the plane folded his arms and leaned against an unoccupied seat. Suddenly, with a grunt, a heavy, florid-faced man only a few feet from him rose to his feet, stumbled, and fell on the hijacker, folding him in a kind of bear hug. "Fuckin' communists!" he was muttering. There was liquor on his breath. Instantly taut as a wire, the terrorist swung his gun hard against the side of the man's head. The assailant collapsed. As he kicked the limp form from him the hijacker whirled to face the whole cabin. He did not shout, he screamed: "Stay in your seats! Hands in the air! Next one that moves I shoot! You want to kill yourselves, you idiots, we'll blow you all to hell!"

It was a very high-pitched scream and it paralyzed every passenger in the plane. People held their hands above them, their faces frozen. At the other end of the aisle the hijacker who had been chatting with the stewardess grabbed her around the neck once again and thrust the gun to her temple. "One more false move and she gets it!" he said. "That was a totally stupid thing to do."

It seemed then that the tension in the plane was even higher than in the first moments after the takeover. The hijacker in the yellow jacket poked his head out of the cockpit, saw the hands in the air, and asked what had happened. "Shithead jumped Peter," his comrade responded.

"Peter shoot him?"

"Slugged him."

"You crazies," he yelled down the length of the plane. "I've got my finger on the button of this grenade. The safety pin's out. I let it go for two seconds and you've had it, every one of you. The whole plane's had it. Shape up!" He ducked through the cockpit door again and jabbed the back of the captain's neck with his pistol. "You've got a goddamn zoo out there trying to get us all killed. Tell them they better straighten out."

The captain's voice came over the loudspeaker. "This is Captain Wald. There must be no attempts—I repeat, no attempts—to interfere with any of these gentlemen in any way during the course of the flight. It is in their power to destroy

*the aircraft and everyone aboard. Please cooperate with them.
We will soon be in Algiers."*

Back in the economy section the hijacker who had knocked
out the attacker permitted passengers to lower their hands.
An old woman several seats in front of him clasped her arms
around her body and shivered. The hijacker eyed her for a
few moments, then reached for a blanket in the overhead rack
and handed it to her.

"Here, lady, put this around you."

"Thank you."

In the forward part of the plane his comrade had released
the stewardess he had seized during the alarm. She asked to
be allowed to use the lavatory and received his permission.
When she came out she saw a look of consternation on his
face.

"Hey, look, that young girl over there. She's crying. That's
no good. There's nothing to cry about. Go talk to her."

The stewardess walked to the seat as if it were a normal
flight and put her hand on the girl's shoulder. She was fifteen
or sixteen and very frightened. "There. It's all right. We'll land
safely. It's all right. Don't cry."

They were already beginning their descent. The captain
had found Algerian authorities highly ambivalent about the
hijacking. They appeared to support the fugitives' desire to
avoid prosecution and receive asylum in their country, but
they were embarrassed by the methods employed and clearly
worried about the repercussions in the international community. To his question about what he should say to the hijackers
the captain had received no clear response.

"It's disappointing that you can't talk with someone who
can give you a straight yes or no answer. Everyone on the
ground had to check with someone else. They couldn't seem
to understand that this guy had his gun at the back of my head
all the while."

As the plane touched the tarmac and taxied to a remote
corner of the airport the passengers seemed to heave a collective sigh. *At least we won't crash to the earth in flames.*

It can't be too much longer now. The hijackers, however, appeared as nervous as before. After the plane cut its engines everybody remained seated. The fat man on the floor came to and a passenger helped him into a seat. Minutes stretched on. Inside the cabin the atmosphere became moist and overheated. Several people wanted to go to the lavatory, but nobody did.

Meanwhile, anxious conversations were taking place between the cockpit and officials in and around the terminal building. The hijackers were aware that police were about; how many and for what purpose they did not know.

"No, we're not just going to walk off the plane. We want hard and fast guarantees. We want asylum in exchange for these hostages. That's the whole point of this mission."

Back came the voice of the negotiator on the ground. "As I said before, our main concern is with the safety of the passengers. We're just trying to make sure that they get out of the airplane OK."

"All right, then—here's what we do. We take two passengers with us to guarantee our safety. You let us out first and give us that car you promised and the rest can come out ten minutes later." Silence at the other end. "OK?" asked the hijacker.

Negotiators in the terminal building were doing their best to interpret the tone of his voice. In that final question they thought they had picked up something. "I'm afraid that wouldn't work," the negotiator responded. "We can't allow the hostage situation to continue. You must come out of the plane first, drop your weapons, go to the car, and then all the passengers will be allowed to leave the plane."

"Bullshit," said the hijacker. "You disarm us and lure us into a trap and that's the end of the game. No thanks. I didn't come two thousand miles to go from one goddamn jail to another."

Had the hijackers at this point injured or killed one of the passengers they might once again have seized the initiative and forced the authorities to cooperate with them. But somehow that did not seem a realistic alternative. They had begun to feel they were bargaining for the lives of everybody aboard the airplane; they were part of a community. Hours passed. Eventually it was decided that two of the hijackers would leave the plane first and go to the waiting car. The third would cover the passengers until they had had time to drive off. Then he would emerge, weapon in hand, and walk to a point at the edge of the airstrip where his comrades would pick him up. No one was to come within range of him or he would begin firing at the plane.

"OK," said the hijacker in the yellow jacket, who broke the news to the passengers in the cabin. "We're going now. You've all been very good. Hang in here with my buddy for a few minutes till we get to the car, then you wait for him to leave, then you can all get out of the plane. Goodbye." He was beaming and he seemed to have trouble with some of his words. Several passengers said "Goodbye." As the two men left they hugged the stewardess who had spent the first part of the flight with a gun at her throat. She hugged them back.

The sequel is anticlimactic and predictable. The getaway worked—up to a point. The third terrorist got off the plane and joined his friends in the waiting car, and the passengers disembarked feeling weak, confused, and in some cases near tears. They were herded into a terminal building where doctors examined them and detectives questioned them. Meanwhile the getaway car, discreetly followed by police, ran out of gas as predicted—the gauge had been wired on the "full" mark— and the hijackers, finding themselves surrounded, chose to give up rather than fight. They too were weak, drained, almost hysterical. They half believed they would be given asylum and not punished for the escapade. The authorities were not sure what they could do legally or should do morally—in the shifting morality of international politics. But that is another story.

† †

Of the available forms of theater, few are so captivating— figuratively as well as literally—as skyjacking. The boldness of the action, the obviousness of the danger, the numbers of people involved as hostages and therefore potential victims, the ease with which national boundaries can be traversed and international incidents created, the instantaneous radio and television linkages—all combine to make this crime one of the most immediately attractive forms of terrorist action. Yet, particularly in recent years when police and airline security officials have learned to cope more effectively with the situation, it is also, as we have seen, one of the most risky ventures for the terrorist. In the long run other forms of forcible abduction will almost certainly prove more effective in turning a small terrorist core into a revolutionary movement. When a terrorist abducts his own compatriots, the essential question is whether the basic pro-revolutionary spark of sentiment exists, waiting to be fanned into flames. Mao Tse-tung's discovery, in China during the thirties, that the peasantry were implacably hostile to their landlords made it hardly necessary to coopt men into the People's Army. By mid-1945 his rural base was strong enough to rout Chiang Kai-shek's Nationalists in just over three years, even though the Nationalists continued to shanghai civilians to replace defections and received a constant flow of American weapons, which they just as rapidly lost to Mao's Communists.

Eight years later, faced with a quasi-militarist official government dominating daily life in Kenya, the Mau Mau movement abducted its members one by one and in an awesome ceremony swore them to loyalty on penalty of death. There were quislings, of course—cowards and informers and people who disagreed on principle—but the evidence indicates that for the overwhelming majority of Kenyans so inducted, the oath-taking ceremony provided an occasion for a recognition of values and motives which most people believed would in the long run be in their best interests. Thus every terrorist kidnapping of this kind potentially serves a double purpose: It removes one member from the controlling society, to the consternation of that society, and it may add a member to the smaller, momentarily weaker, would-be revolutionary movement.

There are, of course, many occasions when kidnapping is carried out with practically no expectation of winning converts. In particular the kidnapping of diplomats or other high officials—of persons who can be expected to be most highly committed to the government that the terrorists oppose—is an attempt simply to exert leverage, exact concessions, and announce to the world that the dissident group is in deadly earnest. The extent to which terrorists and their diplomatic hostages may form emotional alliances that hinder the execution of the group's plans depends on the mental and emotional makeup of the diplomat himself. The better trained he is, the more committed to the aims, principles, and policies of the country he serves—in fact, the more he is able to remain in contact, by telephone or messenger, with his government throughout the ordeal—the less likely he will be to sympathize with either the grievances or the tactics of his captors. Accordingly, the easier it will be for them to kill him. Consequently the current debates that range within the foreign offices of many countries affected by terrorism over whether to have a "tough" or a flexible negotiating policy in the face of diplomatic kidnappings might well be broadened to question whether the diplomats themselves should be trained to adopt a less rigid posture in confrontation with their captors. In a life-or-death situation a relaxing of diplomatic formality in favor of sympathetic responsiveness to the views and the political predicament of the terrorists could, on occasion, save lives. Already aware of this possibility, some terrorist groups have taken steps to ensure that the guards holding diplomatic hostages are changed at frequent intervals, before friendly relations can be formed. However, the need of most such groups to restrict kidnapping operations to a small detail limits the number of "guards" they can deploy, and can force what is for the terrorists' purposes a dangerously high degree of contact.

Clearly, then, planning and strategy based on political realism are critical to the success of a nascent revolution, whether or not its tactics include those forays into violence we call terrorism. Yet in spite of elaborate precautions, rules, and even treatises on the art and technique of terrorism, guerrillas persist in denying final responsibility for their acts in an essentially mystical argument. In his own ideal image of himself the terrorist is an ascetic dedicated to a cause far greater than himself. His arguments take him further, beyond reason: it is the cause rather than the terrorist that determines the tactics. "What are the reasons for so many young men to take up arms and dash people to death—sometimes to lose their own lives doing it?" asked Bassam Abu Sharif. "Do you think Palestinians love to kill? Of course not." It is the opponent rather than the terrorist who determines whether hostages will be killed. "We shall use as little violence as possible to achieve our demands," asserted Busic's Croatian hijackers. (That is, we shall use as much as is necessary.) It is the assassination victim (or his government) rather than the assassin who brings about his own death. Terrorist groups call such killings "executions" on the model of the dominant societies that make the killing of certain outlaws seem the logical end-product of inexorable justice, a punishment by laws, not men. Like that of established governments, the rhetoric of terrorism is curiously capable of representing conscious policy and tactical decisions as *reactions* against hostile forces that lie for the most part beyond the tactician's control. In this way victim and perpetrator are blurred in the public mind—as they may also be blurred in the minds of the participants. In the world of the terrorist, numerically weaker than his entrenched opponent and with only sporadic access to public opinion through the media, words and impressions are more real—and sometimes more deadly—than guns and bombs.

III

HARDENING
THE TARGET

THE WHITE HOUSE IS A HARD TARGET. A TALL WROUGHT-IRON fence runs along the Pennsylvania Avenue side, dotted by guardhouses. If you try to walk through one of the six electronically operated gates, decorated with cast-iron grillwork, you will be detained by guards who will check anything you're carrying with metal-detecting devices. They will examine your credentials carefully, because they're paid to be suspicious. Security officials speak mysteriously of "sophisticated communications and alert systems" and a "secondary perimeter of security" at the White House, but they do not like to give details.

Nevertheless, twice in 1974 the tight security was breached. On February 17, Robert K. Preston stole a U.S. Army Huey helicopter from Tipton Army Airfield in Fort Meade, Maryland and headed toward the capital. On the way the Maryland state police spotted him and took off in two helicopters in pursuit. Preston reached the city, hovered near the Washington Monument, and then flew straight toward the White House. By now the White House guards were alerted. Preston buzzed the mansion several times, then landed on the South Lawn. It was two A.M., but the floodlights were on. Police Cpl. Louis Saffran, who was on the scene, recalled, "I've never seen so many blue uniforms, black uniforms, yellow stripes, and what-have-you. They all came out of the bushes. It was like somebody set fire to an ant colony." Preston's helicopter was greeted by buckshot before it touched the earth. The instant he emerged, guards from the Executive Protection Service jumped him and wrestled him to the ground. He proved to be unarmed.

It was an unnerving time. *The New York Times* commented

with dismay, "Short of enclosing it in a plastic bubble, the White House will always be vulnerable from the air." After that the security people added antiaircraft protection to 'the White House fail-safe system.

That meant that would-be intruders had to go back to basics. On Christmas Day in the same year, Marshall H. Fields crashed his car through one of the gates of cast-iron grillwork at a little after seven A.M. He emerged unhurt from his car to confront the surprised guards, dressed as an Arab and carrying fake explosives, which everyone thought were real. He began speaking in Arabic, but it didn't last. Four hours later he surrendered, after the Howard University radio station broadcast his appeal to meet with Pakistan's ambassador to the U.S., Sahabzada Yaqub-Khan, who politely declined. More than two years later, during the Hanafi Muslim occupation of three buildings in Washington, Yaqub-Khan was to accept a similar offer and become a hero.

The tendency of Americans to focus both adulation and opprobrium on the president makes him at all times the foremost target in the country. Small wonder that the full-time efforts of more than two hundred fifty persons go into "hardening" this target—making it hard to reach and even harder to hit. But because people are notoriously more difficult to guard than buildings, owing to their regrettable faculty for the unplanned and the willful, presidents, despite the best efforts of the Secret Service, may still occasionally be shot. In the history of the United States four presidents (more than one out of ten occupants of that office) have been fatally shot and five others have been shot *at*. Yet in spite of repeated assassination attempts by the alienated, the fanatical, and the demented, no president has ever been shot (or stabbed, strangled, poisoned, or blown up) on the premises of the White House.

It's not a bad record. If we have hopes of keeping political violence from taking its toll through terrorism, we could do worse than study the preeminent science of prevention that is the special province of security agents and bodyguards. "Target hardening," as this science is known, works not by making it less desirable to commit a terrorist act (as, for example, by meting out severe punishments to convicted offenders, a technique of dubious efficacy, as we shall see) but by making it less possible. Its purpose is to demonstrate to the terrorist that his exploit will not work. What it means for a terrorist exploit to "work" depends on the particular operation. Any terrorist activity, however, involves the calculation, "If I do this, then *that* will follow." *That* may be the terrorist's own freedom, the release of political prisoners by a hostile government, a full-blown revolution, or simply publicity for the terrorist's cause. With some insight into this thought process, the strategist who hopes to neutralize a terrorist group seeks to intervene in the chain of cause and effect in order to make sure that *that* never comes to pass. Such intervention can take place at various points in the process of a terrorist act depending on the nature of the act and on its purpose. There are three primary tactics, each applicable at a different point.

Security begins before the act is committed. Preventing the terrorist from even reaching his target is the surest way to prevent the act from occurring. Fences, radar screens, bodyguards, building guards, receptionists, locks, and thick concrete walls are under some conditions excellent security devices. Rigorous procedures for keeping tabs on everyone in a building will minimize the likelihood that intruders can enter to plant explosives or do harm to individuals; on the other hand the freedom of the building's inhabitants to come and go as they please will be correspondingly limited. Like all security measures, including the use of elaborate police forces with extended powers, those used in connection with target hardening have a tendency to inhibit personal rights.

The threat of a counterforce against terrorist activities, particularly guerrilla activities, is the natural second line of defense by a country whose security installations have actually been penetrated. The government of such a country often faces a delicate choice: its response must be strong enough to convince the terrorists that it would be hopeless to pursue guerrilla activity, yet not so massive or overwhelming as either to make martyrs of the guerrillas or to seem to acknowledge the existence of civil-war conditions. Tactical police units are therefore usually favored over military troops for use against internal terrorist and urban guerrilla threats.

The final tactic, *nonnegotiation,* is available specifically with those forms of terrorism that involve hostage taking and, by demanding a response from the affected government, allow the government to choose what that response will be. Tacticians who favor refusal to negotiate with terrorists under any circumstances argue that the likelihood of government capitulation encourages the terrorist in his desperate ploy of threatening innocent lives. If through the risk and quite possibly the loss of some hostages' lives the terrorists are convinced that no matter how grisly the threat their demands will remain unmet, then—so the argument goes—they will stop seizing hostages.

Within each country affected by terrorism, and in the conference rooms of the United Nations, urgent policy debates on the proper choice among these responses testify to the steely precision with which terrorists have probed the bare nerves of the societies they oppose. Controversies arise not only because some of the tactics entail socially unacceptable risks in the nations that would apply them, but because they in fact don't always work. To judge among the alternatives we need to look at each of them in considerably more detail.

"Suppose," said the young architect, "we obtained the plans of the major government and business buildings in San Francisco that were built within the past fifty years. They'd show us the location of ducts and vents for the air conditioning systems in every structure. Nobody could live or work in those buildings without air conditioning: you can't even open the windows. Security isn't that heavy. A small bomb dropped into the right place in each of them would put it out of commission for weeks or months. By doing this systematically we would completely disrupt corporate and government activities in this city."

The speaker was a radicalized professional who during the 1960's seriously considered joining his colleagues in an effective terrorist attack in protest against the United States involvement in Vietnam. This particular attack did not come to pass, but it was eminently feasible. It was feasible because a technological society, like a complex organism, is vulnerable in many of its vital parts. Terrorists and those who would incite them to violence are fond of reciting the ways in which an ordinary man, with ordinary tools, can disable large mechanisms of commerce or government. A train can be derailed simply by loosening the mountings on eight successive ties. A hand grenade (for some activists this is an ordinary tool) tossed into the air intake of a jet engine will destroy the plane. Sand in the gearboxes of freight cars will grind up the bearings. Sugar in the gas tanks of automobiles and trucks will ruin the engines. Explosives or fire can destroy computers, tapes, and records.

Both sabotage and assassination are predicated on the notion of a vulnerable spot, like an Achilles heel, which, if attacked, will quickly disable the oppressive and essentially monolithic society imagined by the terrorists. The problem, of course, is that few societies are monolithic; in the democratic West even a charismatic leader is not the only mainstay of a nation, and rarely does a movement depend on a single figure. In losing John and Robert Kennedy the United States was never seriously compromised as a political entity, however shocked and grief-stricken its people; in losing Martin Luther King, Jr., the black community lost a spiritual focus but little momentum in its drive toward shared power. Similarly, sabotage is likely to have more of a psychological than an economic impact on the target nation, whose industrial resources usually far exceed the terrorists' capacity to destroy them. By contrast, it is the dissidents who stand to suffer most from the assassination of one of their number. Their forces are small; sometimes they are only a handful. Leadership among them, therefore, is in the nature of things a much rarer commodity and its loss correspondingly more catastrophic. International leftist opposition to Stalin's entrenched regime during the thirties, for example, was centered in a relatively small group of people and received its death blow with the assassination of Leon Trotsky in Mexico in 1940.

Yet in spite of the relative resilience of established governments in the face of attacks on persons and property, no one will deny that security measures are necessary and even vital. The stability of nations is predicated on the orderly continuity of institutions, and that continuity can be assured only when leaders can be relied on to lead and agencies to fulfill their appointed functions. Since the first line of defense against disruption of this orderly flow is security, it is hardly surprising to find billions of dollars spent around the world to protect persons and property, quite apart from national budgets for military defense. Yet no amount of money or effort can protect all buildings, persons, or installations all the time. Buildings that must be used by the public, such as air terminals, can be used by terrorists as well. Politicians and candidates, by their nature and the nature of their jobs, will address crowds, shake hands, and smile into cameras and sometimes into the barrels of guns. Refineries, arsenals, and nuclear power plants can be made off-limits to unauthorized personnel and placed under heavy guard, but they can nevertheless be infiltrated, robbed, disabled. A certain vagueness permeates the economics of security: it is clear that after a certain point the benefits derived from increased security do not warrant its costs, but it is not clear when that point has been reached.

There is a further complication: security measures are considered effective not only to the extent that they can ward off terrorist attacks but also to the extent that they provide assurance to the public that they, their leaders, and their vital institutions are being safeguarded. In this sense their symbolic value can vastly exceed their actual value as protective measures. Curiously, potential terrorists, whose choice of methods is often influenced by trends, appear nearly as affected by symbolic security precautions as the general public. The introduction in 1973 of security checkpoints in airports, first in the United States and later around the world, at which hand luggage was X-rayed and passengers were inspected for handguns or explosives, led to a sudden sharp drop in the incidence of airplane hijackings altogether for a period of three and a half years. Yet objectively the problem for the terrorist had not been made insurmountably difficult. Guns were admittedly harder to smuggle aboard an airplane, but nothing in the security procedures prevented passengers from carrying razor blades. A lone hijacker proved that point on a flight from Tokyo in May 1977. He was overpowered, but he might have planned better: five determined terrorists with razor blades at the throats of flight attendants could be as effective as five hijackers with guns or bombs. Nevertheless the hijacking of planes became a significantly less common event. After 1973, hijack attempts declined from a world average of over seventy-two annually during the four-year period of 1969–72 to an average of just over twenty-four per year in 1973–75. Terrorists and the general public were affected both by the checkpoints and by what they symbolized.

Thus in symbolic as well as economic terms the measures initiated by the United States Federal Aviation Administration and instituted throughout much of the rest of the world through American pressure appear to have justified their expense. Currently over three hundred thousand persons are employed at airline security checkpoints around the world and nearly half a billion dollars are spent by airlines annually in maintaining acceptable levels of security. In the United States alone, during 1974 security units arrested 3,501 persons at checkpoints and detected 2,450 firearms, 21,468 knives, and nearly 15,000 explosive devices, including ammunition and fireworks. Fewer people were arrested the following year, but almost twice as many weapons and explosives were detected, indicating either that officers were becoming more chary about making arrests or—more likely—that still more checkpoints were in use and that those hardy individuals who tried to breach them were arming themselves more heavily in the irrational hope of getting something past the X-ray devices.

All such security measures involve a compromise in human rights which the great majority of passengers have suffered gladly in hopes of avoiding trouble during flight. In their various ways travelers and security personnel have tried to humanize the situation, sometimes with unplanned results. It took passengers a little while to realize that even a casual joke about a bomb in one's luggage was cause for arrest, and it took officials even longer to figure out how to deal with such improbable but not unnatural attempts at humor. Ponderously, they evolved guidelines for distinguishing a serious bomb threat from a joke, one of the criteria for "seriousness" being that it should be "impossible to determine immediately if [the threat was] made in a joking manner."

They also muffed a few. Several would-be hijackers boarded airplanes not through airport gates but from the loading ramp after skirting the terminal building altogether. One alert passenger spotted a man who had entered this way sitting in a nearby seat with a six-inch hunting knife on his hip. Security officers arrested him and removed him from the plane before takeoff. Another man who entered by the usual routine tripped the detection device several times when the checkpoint officer repeatedly asked him to walk through it. Finally he lost patience and headed determinedly toward the boarding ramp. Unaccountably, no one stopped him. Then, just as he was boarding the plane, a pistol fell out of his pants leg. Finally galvanized into action, the police and security officers surrounded and arrested him. He turned out to have a leather holster strapped to the inside of his right leg and he was carrying a knife as well.

One of the oddest faux pas occurred during the late weeks of 1972, just before electronic devices were introduced at virtually all airport checkpoints in the United States. At that time all checking was done by hand, and in the first flush of enthusiasm for the new system, determined not to let a single hijacker pass the gate, some of the attendants were conscientious to a fault. One of them almost cost a major United States airline its permit to fly to Italy.

It happened that just before Christmas the Italian ambassador to the United States and his wife were returning to Rome for the holidays. At the Dulles International Airport in Washington they patiently submitted to the rigorous search procedures. (Airlines are not ready to assume that no would-be hijacker will buy a first-class ticket.) All their carry-on bags were explored by hand. This time, when the young attendant pawed through the travel bag of the ambassador's wife, he came upon something totally unfamiliar to him and therefore suspicious. Extracting it from the bag and holding it aloft, he inquired of anyone within earshot, "Now what the devil is this?"

It was an intrauterine device.

Presumably, despite the personal embarrassment (annoying but tolerable to the experienced and the traveled), such an incident, had it befallen the British ambassador's party, would have been unlikely to trigger an international political crisis. However, Catholic Italy, even modern Catholic Italy, was another matter. Caesar's wife, after all . . . There was hell to pay for the airline and for a few days a sense of imminent crisis; but after the dust had settled—*che vuole?*—no permit was revoked. It would have been too hard to explain the whole matter to the press.

On almost all occasions, however, the electronic and X-ray devices, once installed, did what they were supposed to do: they stopped the sinister, the naïve, the ingenious, and the insane impartially whenever one of them tried to walk through the gates carrying a gun or a knife. A woman triggered the device as she came past the checkpoint carrying a paper bag. "Oh, that must be my radio," she said with a disarming smile and handed the bag to the attendant. There was indeed a radio in the bag, but the attendant knew that radios don't make the device go "beep" that way. He opened up the bag and discovered a gun inside.

Another time the device sounded when a man walked through the checkpoint. "Please remove all metal objects from your pockets," the attendant requested. The man took out coins and keys and walked through again.

"Beep."

"Anything else?" asked the attendant. The prospective passenger took eight rounds of ammunition from his pockets and tried again.

"Beep."

"Maybe there's something wrong with the device."

"Try again."

"Beep."

When they finally searched him, they discovered a pistol on the inside of his pants leg, dangling at the end of a string tied to his undershorts.

Most of the people thus apprehended are not prospective terrorists. While their motives vary, many comprise the rather large group of persons who experience varying degrees of psychic disturbance yet are not thought to constitute an immediate or apparent physical threat and so are permitted to go about at large. One young man, stopped by an airport police officer for questioning on the basis of suspicious actions, said that he was planning to follow some passengers aboard a plane, divert it to Peking where life was "pure," and drop a few bombs on the United States along the way to show Americans they were living wrongly.

Another managed to find an unlocked gate near the terminal leading to the aircraft loading area and drove his car through it, parking under the wing of a plane that was boarding. He got out of his car and joined the queue. When a stewardess stopped him, he told her his auto contained explosives and that he was going to steal a ride on the plane. There was a hasty conference among the flight crew, then one of them emerged to tell the would-be hijacker he had to move his car. "Otherwise the plane won't be able to take off, you know." Docilely, he walked down the ramp to do so and was arrested.

Such escapades, such comedies of errors, should not obscure the fact that terrorists, when they succeed in penetrating airport security posts, are deadly serious and are usually intelligent and self-possessed enough to carry through their plans. They are rightly perceived by established governments as a threat, but the nature of the threat is subtler than most officials recognize. Though air travelers seem quite willing to tolerate the inconvenience of being inspected, and the possible compromise of civil rights, in return for the diminished chance of finding themselves aboard a hijacked airplane, other security measures would doubtless be less popular. Police officials complain of the difficulty of keeping tabs on known terrorist agitators in an age of mass transportation and wide freedom of movement. These difficulties vary. In some European countries police are informed of all hotel registrants, with the result that movement from city to city is much more easily scrutinized there than in, say, the United States. This degree of scrutiny is accepted as an ordinary part of life, much as an American accepts having to present his driver's license when an officer requests it; yet it would take a much more apparent terrorist threat than presently exists to convince the majority of Americans that all U.S. hotels should daily report their registrations to the local police departments.

What might arouse American anxiety to new heights is the tangible threat of terrorist access to nuclear installations. The spread of nuclear power plants has raised in many people's minds the bogey of the terrorist who might steal plutonium and use it to construct a bomb with which he could wield the same international leverage now enjoyed by only a few governments. Not just the common misapprehension that most terrorists are deranged gives rise to this fear; many people are uneasy with the knowledge that their own governments have access to such universally destructive power, and they are loath to see it seized by a small cadre of unknown and untried persons, whatever their political orientation or emotional solidity.

Those who can bear to contemplate such matters take small comfort in the daunting physical problems confronting the would-be plutonium thief. Plutonium fuel rods, used in nuclear reactors, are extremely heavy and when encased in the protective lead casks necessary to shield handlers from lethal radiation they often weigh in the vicinity of one hundred tons. Moving one is therefore a major operation, hardly something to be carried out by stealth in the dead of night by a dedicated band of terrorist stalwarts. However, plutonium nitrate $(Pu(NO_3)_3)$, a not very radioactive greenish liquid shipped in barrels, might be stolen and, given the right technology, could be processed to yield bomb-grade plutonium. Some engineers and security officials have proposed that the material be shipped in unrefined or "unpurified" form, which would require exceedingly heavy containers that, again, should discourage even highly enterprising terrorists.

Whether nuclear terrorism is a near reality is still a matter of speculation. What is certain is that nuclear hoaxes have already been tried. It is possible for a bright teenager to consult the right reference works and produce a sufficiently accurate diagram for an atomic bomb to convince authorities that he'd better be taken seriously. On more than one occasion a crude blueprint, specifying the basic nuclear bomb components, has arrived in the mail of a local police department or FBI headquarters and caused a minor scare, only to be revealed as the work of a high school student who had access to some good reference works. But in the fall of 1976 John Aristotle Phillips, a senior at Princeton University majoring in aerospace engineering, designed an atomic bomb for a physics project that earned him an A for the course and led to overtures from a number of foreign governments anxious to see his plans. Phillips wisely kept his secret but observed, "Today a college undergraduate with a basic foundation in physics is capable of doing just what I did." He obtained most of his information from public libraries and guessed at the design of the triggering device which, in the United States, is a classified government secret.

The extent to which nuclear devices would actually be useful to terrorists is a matter of debate. The German political analyst Karl Markus Kreis points out that there may well be an upper limit to the kinds of arms that can be usefully employed by terrorists: "Rationally assessed with limited objectives in view, the political efficacy of the means cannot be measured solely in terms of the degree of destruction achieved. The crucial factor must always be the extent to which it can be put to calculated use. So it is doubtful whether miniature nuclear devices or [biological and chemical weapons] will ever actually be employed by revolutionaries, even though it should not be long before they might gain access to the know-how." But in fact the crucial factor is not destructive capacity but the ability to pose a convincing and terrifying threat. A nuclear device in the wrong hands would seem ideal for that purpose. So far the real prospect of nuclear terrorism remains an idea that causes the imaginative or the farsighted to wake up in the small hours in cold sweat. It is possible; it may happen in our lifetimes; but up to now terrorists have concentrated on more mundane, though still quite effective, engines for twisting arms.

It would be fruitless and interminable to survey all the forms of security anxious or prudent officials have devised to protect persons and property from malice, connivance, greed, delusion, or an ingenious enemy. We have seen enough to know that security not only has an important effect, it also provides occasion for an elaborate dance between the official world and its unsanctioned opponents. If airplane passengers must pass through a screening point and be searched, terrorists will circumvent that point, either by trying to board the plane without passing through the terminal or, as one of the Croatian hijackers of the TWA jet did in 1976, by flashing an airline employee's pass and walking through a service entrance. What terrorists lack in numbers they must make up for in ingenuity. Government authorities, on the other hand, have the advantage of far greater numbers and some decentralization. When agents of Interpol tracked down the terrorist Carlos in Paris and were shot on the spot, they were instantly replaced. If a government building is destroyed, the operations of government will still go on in other facilities. That is not to say that the loss of property and of lives is not a severe moral and tactical setback. Given the right timing, either side can be badly shaken by such a loss. But the hard, uncomfortable point remains: just as an explosion will not destroy a government, so security measures will not stop terrorism. They may set a movement back, cause it to alter its strategies, make it wary and cautious and more furtive than ever; but they will not terminate it for the simple reason that such measures are essentially passive. They do not attack either the immediate manifestations of terrorism or its root causes. The two further stages of target hardening—counterforce and refusal to negotiate—attempt to do that, though as we shall see they too fail in their final purpose of eradicating terrorism.

One might say the most human, though not the most admirable, response to the "declaration of war" made by the terrorist is retaliation in kind: a strong quasi-military raid against the terrorist group that has victimized the innocent. For emotional reasons that have little to do with the final outcome it is a popular response and a frequently urged policy. Sometimes it appears to work. And often it raises more problems than it solves.

In Belfast in the early 1970's, Gerald McKnight interviewed Maire Drumm in her home, all the while watched through a telescopic sight by a British sharpshooter, his rifle trained on the writer from across the street. Maire Drumm was an Irish patriot whose passionate speeches supporting liberty for Northern Ireland had led hundreds of young men to join the Irish Republican Army and lose their lives fighting British troops.

"I've said sometimes to a few of their wives and mothers, to those bereaved: 'Did I do wrong?' In every case they've told me, 'Never blame yourself. He did what he wanted to do.'

"Well, they died like soldiers. People think we want martyrs. We don't want martyrs, we've had them *ad lib* down the years. We don't need them in the cause of Irish freedom. Of course I feel regret that we've lost these boys, and sorrow for their people. But this is their cause as much as mine.

"What we all regret most is the death of innocent civilians. Quite a few times, let me tell you, this has been due to the British forces not acting on warnings, but that's beside the point. I don't like to see civilians losing their lives, and I'm totally indifferent whether they're Catholic or Protestant. That doesn't concern me. . . .

"I've got to be perfectly honest, in the last instance. *I don't care how many British soldiers die. I have no compassion in the world for them.* I know that is an awfully callous thing for a woman to say, but it is my honest belief that they've got to go, one way or the other. If they leave this country, nobody's going to touch them. But . . . Look at them. They come in here, into the greatest Republican Catholic stronghold there is—all of us living in Andersontown are Catholics, and we don't go around shooting each other—so what are they doing here? They say it's 'protecting' us! But we don't *need* their protection. Who is going to touch us?"

Though delayed by some years, the answer to Drumm's rhetorical question was doubly ironic. Someone would indeed "touch" Maire Drumm, yet the British troops would offer no protection whatever. At the end of October 1976 Grandma Venom, as the British styled her, was in a Belfast hospital recuperating from a cataract operation. Down the corridor came three men in white coats, who stopped at her room and looked in at the old woman, her eyes still swathed in bandages. Finding no one else there they pulled out revolvers and, acting in unison, shot Maire Drumm dead in her bed. The militant arm of the Ulster Defence League claimed credit for the killing, the Catholic community mourned her death, and the British ineffectually protested.

Clearly, the British military presence in the six counties that constitute Northern Ireland has done nothing to settle the problems of that country. To the extent that British troops have been touted as the protectors of the Protestant majority against the militant Catholic minority they have only served to further polarize the two religious communities. The merits of the competing claims and charges by Protestants and Catholics have by now become largely irrelevant to the central problem of bringing peace to the strife-torn six counties. What is undeniable is that in its efforts to force a solution to generations of animosity upon a militant minority, the British presence has succeeded only in fueling a civil war which, inevitably, has spilled over into England itself.

The problem is not unique to Ireland. Any government that uses essentially military means to quell a terrorist uprising grants to the terrorists de facto the status of an opposing army and thereby transforms the struggle into a civil or anticolonial war. This may be a low-risk policy if the government knows to a certainty that the popular support of the terrorist group is very low and the terrorist nucleus can be beaten, but a miscalculation or faulty intelligence can be very costly indeed. During the thirties Chiang Kai-shek called his forays against Mao's Communists "bandit suppression campaigns" to downplay their importance with the general public, but clearly the campaigns were full-fledged military maneuvers, and Mao's troops responded to them as such. At one point, in December 1936, Chiang was kidnapped by a group of Chinese leaders that included Chou En-lai. The group came close to killing him on the spot, but Chou intervened, arguing that his leadership was needed at the moment in the common cause against Japan. Chou's eloquence prevailed and the group agreed to spare Chiang's life. During the next dozen years periodic gestures were made toward conciliation and even coalition between Nationalists and Communists, especially after World War II under the encouragement of U.S. General, later Secretary of State, George C. Marshall, but the gauntlet had been thrown down. What small chance there might have been for a compromise with the Communists during their time of relative weakness had been lost in 1934 when Chiang's troops hounded them six thousand miles to Yenan, where they regrouped and began building an invincible base of popular support among the peasants. In 1948 Mao's Communists began their final drive across the Chinese countryside, taking cities and towns along the way. By the early months of 1949 it was all over for the Nationalists, and they fled the mainland forever.

A second danger of military rather than police tactics applied against terrorists arises from the psychology of the soldiers themselves. It's hard to keep battle-weary men from adopting the methods of the terrorists whose actions they are supposed to be suppressing. This is the case particularly when the terrorists represent a particular ethnic or national group which has pitted itself against the dominant society. Terrorist rampages offer a ready excuse for retaliatory raids by the military. In both cases innocent people are killed, but even though the minority groups may suffer proportionately greater losses, the army that ventures into their midst and attacks non-combatants runs a great risk of being branded not only a terrorist unit but a bully, and the minority movement (what's left of it) stands to profit from its position as underdog.

Israel has experienced the problem firsthand. Guerrilla raids across borders have been a characteristic part of the territorial struggle in the Middle East since before Israel existed as a state, so it is hard to speak of one side as an aggressor and another as a defender of territorial integrity, but for both domestic and international consumption Israel has taken pains to characterize its opponents as "terrorists" and its own guerrilla units as "commandos." As long as the targets of the commando units—and the casualties—were wholly military, international opinion appeared ready to accept the distinction; but once the Arab nations realized the propaganda value of calling attention to civilian deaths—or even nonmilitary property loss—resulting from Israeli commando raids, Israel suffered a palpable loss of esteem in the international community. The pattern has been repeated year after year. In March 1968 Israeli troops blew up the East Jerusalem home of Kamal Nammer, a suspected Al Fatah terrorist. Several other homes in the neighborhood were severely damaged, and Jerusalem Mayor Teddy Kollek, visiting the neighborhood, felt compelled to apologize and offer compensation. Later that same month Israel carried out massive raids, involving some fifteen thousand troops, against Jordan, allegedly to stamp out terrorist bases that operated from Jordanian soil. Days later, on March 24, the United Nations Security Council unanimously adopted a resolution condemning Israel. Yet during the following summer Israel conducted one strike after another in Jordan both by land and by air. Ultimately Jordan herself acted to quell the Arab guerrilla units operating on her soil, though whether this was in response to Israel's military action or out of fear that the guerrillas were beginning to develop a quasi-governmental status within the state of Jordan is not clear.

After Arab groups began hijacking Israeli planes in 1968, Israel's own tactics began to take other forms. An attack on an Israeli jetliner in Athens late in 1968 was followed by an Israeli raid on the Beirut airport during which the commandos destroyed thirteen civilian planes belonging to three Arab airlines. In justification for this raid, Israel warned that "Arab governments that allow the activities of sabotage organizations from their territories must know they bear responsibility for terrorist acts." Members of the United Nations Security Council did not accept this rationale any more than established governments commonly accept the assertion of terrorists that an attack on any citizen is the same as an attack on the corruption of official society. On December 31, 1968, the Security Council voted unanimously to condemn Israel for the attack and urge the payment of compensation.

Again in the spring of 1969 Israeli jets bombed Syria and Jordan. This time, on March 26, 1969, Jordan charged that eighteen civilians had been killed by the raids, and again the Security Council voted to censure Israel, with the United States, Britain, Colombia, and Paraguay abstaining. In an oblique sense Israel may have regarded this vote as a propaganda victory, since it was the first since the 1967 war that did not show unanimous opposition to the violation of the ceasefire ending that war. A year later the Security Council passed a similar resolution in response to Israeli attacks on Arab guerrilla bases in Lebanon; this time the resolution calling for "complete and immediate withdrawal" of Israeli forces from Lebanon was adopted 14–0 with only the United States abstaining. Small wonder that Israel felt herself the target of resentment not only through much of the Third World but among the great powers as well. Yet unlike the guerrilla units she attacked, Israel was a member of the United Nations, with a regular army bound by the Geneva Conventions of warfare to refrain from attacks on civilian targets. The difficulty of distinguishing belligerent from civilian targets in a region where terrorism is rife heightens the chance that any military action against terrorism, whether offensive or retaliatory, will itself take on the hallmarks of terrorism. Under such conditions it is easy to lose the role, and the propaganda value, of the moral paragon.

The problem extends beyond the military to undercover "counterterror" agents. One of the most horrifying stories concerns a group of Israeli agents who set out to avenge themselves against a notorious Arab terrorist. They tracked him to an apartment in Paris and gained entry while he was out. Unscrewing the earpiece from his telephone, they inserted a small but powerful explosive device controlled by audio signals. Then they retreated to a hotel across town. That night the terrorist was in bed with his girl friend when the phone rang. He answered on the first ring. As soon as the agents at the other end of the line recognized the voice of their quarry, they sent a special signal along the wire to detonate the charge. Then they hung up, ran down to their car, and raced across town to the apartment. When they got there and burst in the door, they found a girl on the bed screaming hysterically beside the headless body of her lover.

Yet a third hazard awaits the unwary government that responds to what it perceives as a terrorist threat by sending in the troops: this danger is that the tactic may prove successful. In such a case, apparent success may mask a real failure, and winning a battle can put the victors in danger of losing the war. For terrorism, we must not forget, is theater, and the terrorist is concerned with much more than the relatively modest damage he can do to his enemy's troops, leaders, or property. He is playing before an audience. Instant communications have reduced the world to an amphitheater, and on its bloody turf the emperor's gladiators battle with self-chosen representatives of the empire's subject peoples. Unless the crowd—the international media audience—has been moved to ecstasies of bloodthirsty patriotism, it is not likely to turn thumbs down on the victims when the paid, well-trained and well-armed minions move in for the kill. Recognizing this, the terrorist knows it is in his interest to be seen as the underdog and even to lose a few battles with superior forces. "Terrorists try to make the victimizers look like victims," observed Giuseppe di Gennaro in 1976. He knew whereof he spoke; now director of research at the Italian

Ministry of Justice, he had himself been held hostage by terrorists.

Israel once again offers an example. Between World War II and the establishment of the Jewish state in 1948, Jews committed numerous terrorist acts against Britain in an attempt to force the reversal of the British policy of restricting Jewish entry into Palestine, at that time a British protectorate. World sympathy with the Jewish terrorists, fighting a powerful establishment in the wake of the decimation of their people by Nazi Germany, helped to establish the conditions under which Israel could be born. Born in conflict, it remained in conflict with the ancient Arab antagonists of the Jewish people; only now the Jews constituted a state, and their struggle for national survival assumed a different cast when seen against the struggle of displaced Palestinians to regain lands from which they believed themselves wrongly dispossessed. The Jews became the establishment, the oppressors, the perpetrators of war atrocities; and Israel found herself condemned for unjustified aggression in one United Nations resolution after another.

In the United States a combination of brutality, anxiety, and political bungling has resulted in a similar loss of esteem by the government in its contests with dissident groups. "Government," of course, may include such local manifestations as the city of Chicago, whose police force can muster a firepower as impressive as the entire army of a lesser nation. Chicago police became involved on November 13, 1969, in a gun battle with members of the Black Panther Party. Responding to a distress call that complained of Panthers entering a neighborhood in Chicago's South Side, police found themselves (as they later said) fired upon by snipers. A block away from his cruiser patrolman Francis Rappaport was struck by a bullet and died. Police claimed the bullet had come from the gun of Spurgeon Winters, a young black associated with the Panthers, and another patrolman shot Winters and killed him. Whether Winters ever fired on the policemen, or whether he fired first, was never satisfactorily settled.

Ironically, the original distress call had been placed by Winters' sister. Six other policemen were wounded in the fray, and a second patrolman who was shot later died in a Chicago hospital.

If one believes the Panthers were the aggressors in this action, it might be construed as a terrorist raid that met with a "normal," that is, bloody, response from the Chicago police. But the sequel was not a normal response, and its long-range effect favored the Panthers far more than it did either the police department or the city of Chicago.

Three weeks later, on December 4, a contingent from the Chicago police department moved quietly just before dawn to the door of an apartment near the Black Panther headquarters. Accounts conflict: there may or may not have been a knock at the door. But in any case the next minute the apartment was ablaze with gunfire. Bullets pierced the door and ricocheted off walls, floor, and ceiling. In a few moments over two hundred shots were fired. When the guns finally ceased, Fred Hampton, the Illinois chairman of the Black Panthers, was dead in his bed, and Mark Clark, a Panther leader from Peoria, was dead too. Four other people, two of them women, were wounded. The police suffered no casualties.

No one ever managed to prove either the police's contention that they had knocked at the door only to be answered by a burst of shotgun fire or the Panthers' contention that this was a "search and destroy mission" and that Hampton was murdered in his bed. Certainly the timing of the raid in relation to the earlier battle, and the fact that the two Panther deaths offset the two police deaths, appeared neat enough to have been planned. Sympathetic journalists tended to agree with the Panther claim that the evidence from bullet holes proved that most if not all the shots had been fired by the police. The following January, seven Black Panthers who had survived the raid were indicted by a Chicago grand jury on charges of attempted murder. Yet only a few months later, on May 8, 1970, all seven were freed and criminal charges dropped; State Attorney Edward V. Hanrahan admitted that no one had come forward with sufficient evidence that any one of the suspects had fired a weapon at the police. More than a year afterward, on August 24, 1971, the Illinois Supreme Court ordered the publication of an indictment prepared some months earlier in which Hanrahan and thirteen other law enforcement officials, including eight policemen who took part in the raid and four others who investigated it after the fact, were named on charges of conspiring to obstruct justice in connection with the episode, of planting false evidence, and of conspiring to obstruct the Panthers' legal defense. They were acquitted the following October after a trial during which testimony indicated that four of the Panthers had given written statements to their lawyers contradicting their testimony that they had not fired at the police.

In the morass of charges and countercharges it would have been impossible to prove the facts of the case to everyone's satisfaction. But whatever the true facts were, clearly the police lost the propaganda battle to the Panthers through taking the initiative and conducting a quasi-military maneuver against them. Later on we will encounter a number of other reasons why it is preferable to treat every terrorist action as a common crime rather than a declaration of war by a hostile power.

But suppose the hostile power declares war first? Suppose he makes his move, throws down his challenge, and dares you to walk away? The terrorist challenge is so contrived that the government that ignores it will not merely lose face, it will lose lives. What, in short, should be the response of the government whose nationals have been kidnapped and held hostage, whose lives can be ransomed only by significant concessions that may have serious political and diplomatic repercussions and, most importantly, may show the nation to be an easy mark for future kidnappings and extortions?

With the burgeoning of extortionate terrorist crimes during the sixties and early seventies a growing chorus of voices took up the refrain, "No negotiations with terrorists." The slogan was put forward as national policy in a number of countries, notably the United States and Israel. Like many policies, it was based on an untried theory—namely that terrorists learn by example, and that a threatened power's absolute refusal to respond to demands backed up by a bomb or a bullet will convince other potential terrorists that it would be hopeless for them to pursue a similar course. Conversely, officials often feared that any appearance of softness, any yielding to terrorist demands, would encourage others to make similar demands and would demonstrate the nation's vulnerability and lack of self-confidence. One problem, of course, is that it is very hard, over the long term, to appear less vulnerable than you are.

Israel learned this during the Entebbe hijacking episode in July 1976. The small nation's susceptibility to both military incursions and terrorist attacks had convinced the Israeli government that only a stance of utter inflexibility toward terrorist demands could reduce the long-term threat to national security. Writing about the problem for a Hebrew University symposium held a year before the Entebbe episode, Yehezkel Dror urged a "readiness to accept pain" in the face of what he called "T.F.B.," for terrorism, fanaticism, blackmail. "A credible image of disregarding T.F.B. or accepting it as one accepts traffic accidents and disease, can help a lot to reduce T.F.B. in the longer run. But it requires a readiness to pay an immediate cost and, possibly, an intermediate cost of escalated T.F.B. which tries to break through the pain-threshold. Also, given a concrete society, it is not easy to influence the readiness to accept pain. But when T.F.B. becomes endemic, this is a main effective counter-measure, which can be followed by resolute political leadership which understands the matter." Yet "resolute political leadership" in all but the most totalitarian states is responsible willy-nilly to the will of the people, and sufficient public pressure brought to bear on government at a moment of crisis can change overnight the effective policy, if not the stated one.

Early in July 1976, as the hostages aboard the Air France jet hijacked to Entebbe airport in Uganda sweated out the hours and days in the crowded airport lounge, guarded by armed terrorists inside and armed Ugandan troops outside, dozens of relatives of the Israeli captives gathered outside the iron gates of the Defense Ministry building in Tel Aviv. Tension ran high. The demonstrators tried to force their way inside the building, military police fired a shot into the air, and at least one MP was beaten by the agitated crowd. Memories of the proud inflexibility of earlier times brought the captives' relatives near to panic. Now they urged, "We want the government to do everything possible to free our children and, if necessary, pay whatever need be paid." And the government, which had not always held to the policy of nonnegotiation but had exchanged Palestinian guerrillas for Israeli hostages on hijacked airliners in 1968 and 1969, this time listened and acceded.

"The government of Israel would be ready to start negotiations through the intermediary of the French government and in common with the latter for the liberation of all the passengers in exchange for a certain number of prisoners in Israel," said the Israeli embassy in Paris. For the next day or so the captives and their kin lived on the hope that an exchange would be made and all would be well.

In the light of the final outcome of the Entebbe episode it is possible to suspect that the apparent capitulation was a calculated move by the Israeli government, that officials never really intended to negotiate and were using the ploy to buy time. But it is hard to perceive the difference between such a ploy and that of any other armed negotiator in a desperate situation. Negotiation *is* buying time. In the desperate game of terrorism with its high stakes and minimal rules, either opponent may feel justified at any moment in aiming a lethal blow at the other, negotiations or not. But neither opponent can be sure that a forceful move on his part will succeed, or even that he will be able to bring it off. The sharpshooter keeps his sights trained on the kidnapper, but the kidnapper is smart and afraid and keeps the hostage's head next to his own at all times. As long as he does so, the bullet meant for him will never leave the chamber. Meanwhile, the officers on the ground negotiate. They're buying time, and they might eventually get somewhere: someone's guard will relax, someone's nerve will snap. The likelihood is that Israel's attitude was similar. It would negotiate and, if necessary, yield its prisoners to regain its nationals, but it would not and could not trust the good will of its opponents. As time went on and the hijackers' demands escalated under the baleful influence of Ugandan president Idi Amin, it became plain to the strategists that a rescue attempt offered more hope of success than their conciliatory posture. But the negotiations, nevertheless, were real and under other circumstances might have led to an exchange of "prisoners."

Attitudes toward this form of target hardening vary, depending on who is being threatened. Four years previously, in 1972, in response to demands by the hijackers of a Lufthansa jet, the West German government released three of the Arabs who had taken part in the Munich slayings of Israeli athletes two months before. At that time the Israeli government charged the Germans with lack of will and urged that "every capitulation encourages the terrorists to continue their criminal acts." Israeli Foreign Minister Abba Eban protested through diplomatic channels against this "capitulation to terrorists" and questioned whether there had been "a change in German policy regarding terrorists and their actions." The West German government replied that Eban seemed to have missed the point that twenty lives were at stake, but the American State Department criticized the German decision too, and expressed "regret that known terrorists can secure their freedom as a result of extortion and blackmail and can find safe haven." *

Yet only months after the Entebbe hijacking the United States found itself faced with demands from the Croatian nationalists who hijacked a Chicago-bound TWA jet and forced it to fly to Paris. In the wake of this new episode the State Department protested that its hard-line policy had been misunderstood. "We will not negotiate with terrorists" really means "We will do everything to effect the safe release of

---

* Fifteen months later, in Mogadishu, Somalia, the West Germans imitated the Israeli tactic and stormed a hijacked Lufthansa jet to free eighty-six hostages, in the process killing three of the four terrorists aboard. World reaction was overwhelmingly favorable.

hostages without making any concessions," according to the department. Others pointed out, however, that talking to terrorists is itself a concession, as most certainly is the dropping of leaflets they have printed and the publication of their manifestos in major newspapers. Yet the American government's expressed position clearly had caused as much terror among the passengers and crew of the jetliner as the terrorists themselves. "Tell me, please, what are we being killed for?" asked Captain Richard Carey over his radio as the plane stood on the runway in Paris. And a little later, on the edge of breakdown, he observed tremulously to U.S. ambassador Kenneth Rush, who was in the control tower of the Charles de Gaulle Airport, "All we know is that these people had a message that they wanted to put in the papers and wanted to drop leaflets on cities, and for this you are asking that this whole ship full of innocent people can be killed to prove that you can take a stand against terrorists."

Perhaps the hard line is justified after all. Perhaps, in fact, the proper response to hostage taking is not negotiation but attack, as the Israeli commandos attacked the Air France hijackers at Entebbe. But it doesn't always work, and the failures can be disastrous enough to give any government pause. In 1974 after Arab terrorists had captured the school at Ma'alot and threatened the lives of the children and their teachers, Israel at first planned to negotiate. But communications were poor, somebody panicked, and the order was given to storm the school. Within minutes twenty-one children were dead of terrorist bullets.

The problem is that the usual rules of diplomacy do not apply when a government is faced with a terrorist threat. Diplomatic negotiations are partly bluff, and bluff depends on a degree of uncertainty. In ordinary warfare, in spite of intelligence estimates one is not sure just how effective or how ready the enemy's striking force is, how disposed he is to use it on a particular occasion, or how impressed he is by one's own show of strength. By contrast, a hostage-holding situation like an airplane hijacking is designed to make it very difficult for a government to bluff. The terrorist's strength is known (or at least must be assumed to be as he states it); the amount of damage he can and probably will do if his demands are not met is chillingly easy to estimate. Because he has seized the initiative it is not possible to threaten him with a first strike—with an attempt to destroy him before he can destroy you—for he already holds the power of life or instant death over scores of your people and he can, if he chooses, even now begin killing them off one by one. For these reasons the reverse of the "velvet glove" approach seems recommended: in the absence of an immediate threat, rather than gentle statements of policy and principle backed up by the implied threat of force, one makes the statements sound fierce and uncompromising, hoping that at least some potential terrorists will be deterred. But when the crunch comes and a plane is hijacked, the safest policy is to negotiate, whether covertly or overtly, so as to buy time; for time, as we have seen, is nearly always on the side of the government, not the terrorist. So within the United States State Department the official hard line is often tempered in practice by pragmatic moves at least to discuss terrorist demands, and within agencies less consistently on view, such as the FBI, such pragmatism has become de facto policy.

But not always. The United States has a notably spotty record in negotiations with terrorists involving kidnapped American diplomats or other officials. In eight years, from 1968 to 1975, about thirty American officials were kidnapped by terrorists. Six of these, or 20 percent, lost their lives. Coincidentally, statistics indicate that a terrorist involved in a kidnapping has about a 20 percent chance of being captured or killed. It has not been demonstrated that this figure, which is remarkably low to begin with, would be still lower (that is, that more terrorists would go free) if the United States government were to negotiate with more alacrity when its officials are threatened. But so far American decision makers have preferred nonnegotiation along with the other forms of target hardening as preventive measures: They have tightened security around embassies in major capitals to such an extent that terrorists tend to avoid them and concentrate on embassies in more out-of-the-way places where officials are not always guarded around the clock.

None of this has made career diplomats very happy. The American Foreign Service Association has formed a Committee on Extraordinary Dangers to negotiate with the State Department for a change in policy that would save more lives. Whether such a change occurs will not be discernible from public announcements; it is virtually certain that the official policy will remain the "tough" one. But covert negotiations may take place more often, if they can be carried on without appearing to signal that the United States is an easy mark. "In general," said a spokesman for the West German delegation to the United Nations in the fall of 1976, "you should take a hard line. But don't say 'never.' You can always make room for special cases."

This is not to suggest that terrorist killings are other than an unmitigated evil. But they are at times an avoidable evil, and the power to avoid them lies often with the threatened government. A quick response is not a capitulation. Buying time may be nerve wracking, but it is usually a successful ploy. What evidence we have certainly does not suggest that the mere act of negotiating will increase the frequency of later terrorist attacks, or conversely, that refusal to negotiate will turn terrorists' attention to targets from other nations. During the five-year period when Israel refused categorically to negotiate with hostage takers her nationals were nevertheless the victims of sporadic terrorist attacks both on their home soil and in numerous other countries. The convinced and passionate terrorist will make his point; in the long run no target can be too hard for him.

Meanwhile, a policy of rigid refusal to negotiate may actually harm the country that hews to it—domestically as well as internationally. The government that consistently appears unconcerned with the lives of its threatened citizens, even with the excuse that such an attitude will in the long run *protect* citizens, may find its power base threatened as soon as people feel that an essential sympathy for their plight has been lost. On a more modest scale, specially affected groups can refuse cooperation with governments that seem to take a cavalier attitude toward threats on their lives. Airline pilots, who have already shown the power of concerted action in refusing to fly into countries without airport security checkpoints, thus forcing the virtually worldwide adoption of this method of target hardening, might equally refuse to fly into any country whose demonstrated policy is an unwillingness to negotiate with airplane hijackers under any circumstances.

Not only might citizens react against their own government under such circumstances, they might find their sympathies with the terrorists growing, for reasons discussed in the previous chapter, to such a point that it becomes easy to see the terrorists as a beneficent force, in contrast with an implacable and apparently hostile government. In its futile and unending war with terrorists the Italian government has discovered this discomfiting truth time and again. Lower-class youths in trouble with the law find government officials mainly unconcerned and relatively powerless, while from so-called terrorist gangs they receive money, legal help when arrested, and a sense of belonging. Little wonder that in time many of them come to join the terrorist ranks against provincial or national governments.

In order to retain its mandate a government must continue to appear concerned with the condition of its people. As soon as this concern ceases to be apparent, whether because the people are not "important" economically or socially or because a policy of nonnegotiation is so firmly held that loyal citizens are sacrificed, a certain loss of trust in government responsiveness sets in. At that point it becomes prudent to reassess policy, perhaps to question the assumption that terrorism can really be discouraged by a refusal to comply with well-publicized demands that were carefully designed in the first place to put the government on the spot in the eyes of its own people. It is well to remember that between government and terrorists the real battle is political, whether its mode is a show of quasi-military force, a bit of deftly managed theater, or a combination of the two.

For that very reason policy makers would be naïve to believe that one or another form of target hardening actually solves a terrorist problem. At best such a ploy can work against only those who were not serious terrorists, with well-articulated social grievances and social programs, to begin with. For regardless of its immediate effects, target hardening is essentially a short-term solution, as are all "tough" solutions to social problems. Like other such solutions it reckons without the resilience of the "enemy." Terrorists, like anyone else, can be temporarily demoralized, scared, or suppressed. But it is unsafe and unwise to regard terrorism as a mental aberration among a relatively small group of people who, if shot down or imprisoned, will no longer pose a threat to the public order. Terrorists are not just "them," they are most of us. We have, unfortunately, ample evidence that the capacity to do harm to one's fellow man is widespread and not merely latent in the human species. Usually but not always it expresses itself under official sanction. Stanley Milgram's experiments at Yale are a perversely eloquent form of that evidence. Milgram's subjects, ordinary people with no notable aberrations in their backgrounds, believed they were participating in an experiment about learning behavior. They controlled a console which, they were told, could administer electric shocks of progressively higher force to persons in the next room—out of sight but not out of earshot—who were to be "punished" for giving wrong answers to questions on a test. Despite the screams of agony from the next room, and despite their own profound discomfiture, two-thirds of Milgram's subjects were capable of turning the dial up until it indicated a voltage just short of lethal. The torturer, it appears, lurks in most of us and needs only a little encouragement, and some social license, to emerge and act.

How little encouragement was demonstrated again in Utah in the late fall of 1976 when the end of the nine-year moratorium on capital punishment in the United States was only weeks away. Gary Gilmore, sentenced to die by the firing squad for killing a motel clerk, surprised the nation when he appeared before the judge to ask that legal efforts to stay the execution be ended. "The sentence is proper," he said, "and

I'm willing to accept it with dignity, like a man. I hope it will be carried out without any delay." Had matters been left up to some of Gilmore's free fellow citizens it certainly would have been. So many people phoned the prison volunteering to serve on the five-man firing squad for $175 that selecting among them became a major job. Many callers communicated their passion over the telephone, to the point where warden Samuel Smith announced that he would have to screen out those whose motives appeared "unhealthy" to him, a task that would no doubt have dumbfounded Milgram: how does one look for healthy motives for serving on a firing squad?

Both of these instances point to a human propensity toward violence, a love of killing and torture that emerges when circumstances give such actions the color of legitimacy. In the course of its history, society has found ways to restrict (though practically never to eliminate completely) the occasions for legitimate violence. Those who eschew violence even when the legitimized occasions are clear and unmistakable are still in the minority. It follows that the terrorist differs from the upright and law-abiding citizen not in that he is violent while the citizen is not, but in that the occasions he seizes for his violence are those that society as a whole regards as illegitimate. The essential difference is one not of motive but of politics. It is the terrorist's conviction that the occasion for his violence *is* legitimate because it is sanctioned not by an actual society but by his vision of society. Ordinary war pits soldiers from one state against those from another. Terrorist struggle pits the members of a state that is not yet born—a state of mind—against the members of a state with recognized territory and an official history. That the terrorist should attack noncombatants is deplorable but not really surprising—for his state has not been recognized, and official war has not been declared against him. Each terrorist act, then, is a declaration of war on behalf of a society not yet brought into being.

It should be clearer now why target hardening can be good tactics but poor policy. It is a protective and sometimes a threatening device, but it does not deal with either the motives or the social attitudes of the terrorist, and thus does not really allay the danger he poses. Usually, in fact, it results in the phenomenon social scientists call "displacement." The particular terrorist tactic under siege is abandoned in favor of another with a better likelihood of success because aimed at a more vulnerable spot. After authorities cottoned onto letter bombs and became adept at intercepting them before they could reach their intended victims, terrorists found other ways of making their point. They hijacked planes, kidnapped athletes, murdered civilians. Later, when worldwide security measures made skyjacking much more problematic, terrorists turned to kidnapping diplomats. And just when Americans were becoming sanguine that the skyjacking problem had been solved—in their country at least—five Croatian nationalists demonstrated that skyjacking was still possible, and might have an even greater effect since it was no longer routine but carried much of its old shock and horror. So target hardening serves mainly to displace one form of terrorism by another; the terrorist himself remains as resolute as ever and the struggle continues on other turf.

IV

FEAR AND TREMBLING: THE HOSTAGE GAME

ON THE MORNING OF SEPTEMBER 21, 1976, ORLANDO Letelier, onetime foreign minister in the government of Chile's Salvador Allende, set out from his home in Washington, D.C., toward the Trans National Institute where he worked. With him were his colleagues Michael and Ronnie Moffitt. Letelier drove along fashionable Embassy Row and entered a traffic circle. It was 9:35. The next instant a thunderclap inside the car sprayed glass and metal sixty feet in every direction. The car went out of control and rammed into a Volkswagen parked on the street. Michael Moffitt was thrown from the car, badly hurt but alive. Inside the car his wife was mortally injured. Orlando Letelier was dead.

The grisly episode, apparently the work of terrorist agents of Chile's ruling military junta, was over in a moment, leaving a growing circle of shocked bystanders and the grim police and medical attendants who had the job of cleaning up and investigating. There was no time to argue with the perpetrators, to negotiate, make concessions, respond to demands. Death is absolute.

So it is with the destruction of buildings and factories, the bombing of cities, and the assassination of persons. But hostage-taking episodes are in a different class. They are used to demand a specific reciprocal action, such as the freeing of prisoners or the publication of propaganda. The victims may still be saved, and because of this they become the focus of a tense and often prolonged struggle between the terrorists and the representatives of the larger society. Not surprisingly, the struggle generally takes the form of a dialogue. Strung out on a thin line of words are the lives of every man, woman, and child in the terrorists' power. If words can work miracles, there is no better occasion than this; and who has not dreamed of finding the right formula, the *magic words*, to convince the kidnapper that he should free his captives? Small wonder that everyone wants to be the negotiator: in his heart of hearts each witness to the event is convinced that he could do the job best.

Because hostage taking is predicated on some sort of response from the victimized government, it is unique among the genres of terrorism in requiring not just a stance (such as police protection or target hardening) but a strategy. Alternatives must be weighed rapidly and choices implemented decisively. Who should negotiate, what should be conceded, who should make the decisions, what alternate strategies, if any, should be pursued while negotiations are going on— these are some of the questions that come into play as soon as the terrorist points his gun and announces his demands. In order to deal with him we need a system and some terminology. Let us call the hostage the secondary victim and the group with whom the terrorist negotiates—government, corporation, family, or whatever—the primary victim. The variables—the things that can change from one hostage-taking episode to the next—are both situations and persons. Among the persons the important variables are the hostage taker himself, the primary victim, and the secondary victim.

Everything depends on the outcome of the negotiations, and since neither side has complete control, and each has incomplete knowledge of the resources available to the other, "victory" for either side depends on that side's ability to second-guess its opponent. As yet there is no all-purpose strategy for negotiation. But people who have searched for such a strategy have given more than passing attention to game theory. The plaything of mathematicians and military think tanks, game theory might be called the science of second-guessing. It relies on a presumption most experts are willing to make in the case of the terrorist: that an opponent's decisions will be rational from the point of view of his own self-interest. Given certain assumptions regarding available options—weapons, outside accomplices, the friendliness or hostility of the country in which the episode takes place, the endurance of the principals (terrorists and hostages), and the effect of public sentiment on the primary victim—the marginal benefits of each available choice can be formulated in mathematical terms, and if both sides are operating on the same set of assumptions they will both recognize the option which strikes the fairest compromise—the one with minimal losses—for both sides.

Such precise reasoning may be more likely to occur in the conference rooms of the RAND Corporation or the Pentagon than in an airport control tower a hundred yards from a planeload of frightened passengers and overwrought hijackers. However, the elegant simplicity of the mathematical approach charms the theorist. In the spring of 1976 I attended a conference on hostage taking held in Santa Margherita, Italy. During a stroll through nearby Portofino, Reinhard Selten, professor of mathematics at the University of Bielefeld in West Germany and one of the conference delegates, broached with a mild amusement his ideal approach to the problem of the hostage taker. "Everyone knows," he said, "that once a kidnapper has shot his last hostage he has no more leverage against his primary victim. The police will rush him and if he is not killed resisting arrest he will be put to death by court order or imprisoned for life. So the rational hostage taker knows he must never shoot his last hostage. In that case the last hostage is safe." I nodded as we walked up a hill toward an ancient church. "But suppose a man has seized twelve hostages," Selten continued, puffing. "He cannot kill them all or he will be defenseless. He cannot kill all but two either, for to then shoot the next-to-last hostage would leave him with only one, and we have already seen that he cannot kill the last hostage, so there is really no point in having that last hostage. But in that case"—his breath was coming faster on the steep hill—"if two hostages left offer no protection, neither would three, for to kill one of them would leave only two, which is of no use because to kill the next to last would leave only one, which is of no use for reasons we've already seen. And so on. That line of reasoning should make it plain to the hostage taker that he can't kill a single one of his twelve hostages. Mathematically, his hands are tied. He might as well give up!" This in triumph at the top of the hill.

It was a nice academic joke, and it depended on our ignoring the unlikelihood that a government or corporation would stand quietly by while twelve of its people were put to death one by one, waiting till the hostage taker had exhausted his resources. Clearly game theory, if it is to have any application to this branch of terrorism, must take into account quite a few more variables than Professor Selten mentioned in his little fiction.

In fact a theory that might suffice has yet to be developed, in large part because the variables are still being listed and debated. But we can make a start at surveying them here, beginning with the personal variables surrounding the hostage taker and his secondary victim—the person at whose head the gun is pointed.

The mythology surrounding terrorists, fostered by their victims and supported and embellished by the media, does little to clarify the thought processes behind terrorist actions. To speak of terrorists as *The New York Times* has spoken of the Baader-Meinhof group in West Germany, as "a few fanatic apostles of violence," makes them appear at once utterly threatening and utterly incomprehensible. If we take such a phrase literally we imagine people for whom violence is an end in itself, who aim to destroy not just a particular society but all society; such people are essentially anarchists. (We may then be confused to find Conor Cruise O'Brien, in a discussion of terrorism, speaking of those who *renounce* all use of violence as anarchists.) Are terrorists then nothing but members of the loyal opposition? The truth is not so simple. In virtually every manifestation we have experienced, terrorism sustains itself not by a love of violence, though violence is matter-of-factly used as a tool, but by means of a program. The program may be politically simplistic and naïve, as when members of the Baader-Meinhof group announce their aim to rid the world of capitalism, or the Symbionese Liberation Army forces a food giveaway program as a means of starting a grass-roots revolution among California's poor, but it may also be plausible and ultimately within reach, as was the goal of the Mau Mau to free Kenya from British colonial rule or the strategy of the Algerians and the Viet Cong against the French and the Americans respectively. RAND's Brian Jenkins sums up, "Terrorists want a lot of people watching and a lot of people listening, not a lot of people dead."

Interviews that have been preserved with people who fit our general definition of "terrorist," and the comments such people have volunteered to describe their motivation, tend to confirm this impression. Fayez A. Sayegh, a member of the PLO National Council, explicitly links terrorist actions with specific Palestinian political aims: "The success of the recent Palestinian terrorism in calling the attention of an otherwise indifferent world to the plight of the Palestinian people constitutes an indictment of the conscience of the civilized world." But having achieved its ends, such terrorism, he believes, is in decline. "Born in desperation, the terrorism of the Palestinians lost its motivation as soon as the world became alive to the tragedy of Palestine and aware of the need to restore the rights of the Palestinian people." It is not necessary to agree with either the politics or the methods of the PLO to recognize that Sayegh's explanation is couched not in military but in theatrical terms. Terrorism as he sees it is essentially an attention-getting device. And though other remarks of this PLO theorist indicate that there is also an element of revenge in Arab violence (in that Arabs see it as a response to the provocation of Zionist terrorism), there is no evidence that such actions issue from demented minds, from criminals intent on personal gain, or from the cynical professional hit man.

This support of the theatrical function of terrorism, which could be greatly enlarged with quotations from the Irish Republican Army, the Croatian nationalists, the Basques of Spain, and many others, suggests useful boundaries for our image of the person likely to be a terrorist, and an interesting range of variation in some of its dimensions. The hostage taker who is a genuine political terrorist is unlikely to be capricious or irrational. He is also unlikely to be affected by appeals to personal selfish interests: that is, he cannot usually be bought off. He is conscious of the high risks he takes in his exploits, but he does not protect himself from danger in the way that either a criminal or a policeman might.

Yet for all that he is a professional. He is dedicated to his job and, though he may want very much to avoid dying, he knows he may have to. His immediate resources may be small —he may, in fact, be unarmed, though more likely he is well armed—and he is probably not going to be rescued from a tight spot by sudden reinforcements. If he has taken his hostage to a secret hideout he has an immense advantage over his pursuers, so long as his location remains secret, for he cannot be readily trapped, and he can use his control over the hostage's life to bargain not for his own safety but for concessions that will further his revolutionary program. Once he is hunted out, however, the entire game is changed. So as long as no one knew where the SLA had hidden Patty Hearst the kidnappers were in a position to demand and get a multimillion dollar food giveaway program; had they been discovered the balance of power would have shifted at once: they would have been put in the position of a besieged fortress—still holding real power in the form of their hostage's life, but now forced to wield that power solely to save themselves from capture and meanwhile dependent on the mercy of their opponents for the basic necessity of food.

All of these considerations pass through the mind of the terrorist trying to outwit and outbluff his primary victim. Frightened though he may be, he is still rational. He can be reasoned with, provided two conditions are fulfilled: he must feel able to trust the person he deals with and he must be convinced that there is something to reason about. These two conditions have major implications for the appropriate behavior on the part of the primary victim and his representatives.

First, the negotiator must be chosen not on the basis of how much authority he has in the hierarchy of the victim's political, social, or professional structure but on his ability to instill confidence in the hostage taker. This principle has consequences that we will shortly explore in some depth. Second, the government (or corporation or family) that wishes to conduct real negotiations must make very sure the hostage holders understand that concessions and adjustments of position are possible. Of course, it is entirely reasonable for a government to draw a line at the commencement of negotiations beyond which it will not go. A country may be, and often is, willing to negotiate safe conduct for the terrorists to another country but unwilling to discuss the freeing of certain political prisoners whom it holds. It may be willing to publish revolutionary manifestos but not to pay ransom money. It may, in fact, be willing to yield precious little in return for the release of the hostages, but it must be willing to yield something if negotiations are to be conducted at all. To refuse all negotiations at the outset of a hostage-taking episode may or may not make an impression on other potential hostage takers and thereby lead over the long term to a reduction in terrorist episodes, but it is almost certainly a recipe for disaster in the here and now. "Sir Robert Mark [commissioner of London's Metropolitan Police] believes in waiting, too," says veteran negotiator Frank Bolz of the New York City Police Department, "but he doesn't negotiate; he contains the scene and says, 'Come out when you're ready.' That's wrong."

This point has not been lost on other law enforcement officers. Police or military personnel who have chosen in the past to attack rather than negotiate have usually found the resultant costs unacceptably high. Even if the attack succeeds in obtaining its immediate objectives it usually does considerable damage to the reputation of the attacking force. So the troopers who put down the Attica prison riot in 1971 at the cost of over forty lives won for themselves and Governor Nelson Rockefeller, who ordered the attack, not praise but obloquy. Public sympathy with the prisoners' cause was stirred by the episode; and among the large number of his constituents sympathetic to the prisoners' grievances, the governor's popularity suffered lasting damage. If the attack does not succeed in saving the hostages the result may appear futile to many, even though the terrorists are destroyed.

Thus even cleverly managed Israeli propaganda was not able to obscure the magnitude of the disaster at Ma'alot, where twenty-one children died and sixty-five others were injured in May 1974 as a direct result of a panicky charge by Israeli soldiers against Arab captors. It is easy to be confused by the issues in such cases. True, twenty-one children died at the hands of the Arabs—children who would not have been threatened had the terrorists not adopted the desperate measure of holing up in a schoolhouse. But once the hostages were seized and the ugly situation had been established, it was still possible to avert a major tragedy, and the failure to avert it must be charged against Israel: when a code word failed to arrive signaling the release of twenty Arab prisoners in response to the terrorists' demands, the troops gave up the possibility of negotiation and rushed forward, firing their weapons. After the shooting stopped, all three hostage holders were dead. So were sixteen children. Five others died later from their wounds.

For these reasons even police forces now often prefer to adopt negotiating tactics with hostage takers rather than charge the hideout (assuming they can locate it) with weapons blazing. Faced with nearly two hundred hostage-taking situations annually in major American cities during the sixties, police forces in about fifty cities adopted Strategic Weapon and Tactics (SWAT) squads to deal specifically with hostage-taking situations. In a few years the squads have spread to some three thousand police departments, and many forces have come to pay more attention to tactics than to weapons. The SWAT team in Los Angeles, for example, claims to have fired only five rounds of ammunition over a five-year period,* and those five rounds were fired on only two occasions. The

---

* The attack on the Los Angeles hideout of the SLA in May 1974 was carried out not by the Los Angeles police but by the Los Angeles County force. Considerably more than five rounds were fired on that occasion.

rest of the time, in common with many other units forced to confront terrorist kidnappings, they talked.

How one talks to a terrorist can be a life-or-death matter. Police teams that deal with hostage takers have learned to stay away from the negotiator who is perfunctory or antagonistic. The terrorist hostage taker is not irrational and does not need to be "humored," but he is in a state of heightened sensibility and anxiety and he is unlikely to be very trusting; small displays of irritation on the negotiator's part may easily have a catastrophic effect. Accordingly, such teams will steer away from the kind of police negotiator who feels the way to deal with a threatened suicide is with pressure and a get-tough approach: "I get off duty at five. Either give me that gun or go ahead and blow your brains out." Or the one who says to another suicide standing on the edge of a bridge, "If you jump I won't give you the satisfaction of committing suicide. I'll shoot you on the way down!" With terrorists there can be no trickery. There can be very little humor. Nor will the used-car-salesman type do. The opposing sides must have absolute faith in the negotiator's integrity, if not in each other's.

Who does the talking can be equally important. There are no hard-and-fast rules. A plumber may prove to be a more successful negotiator than a psychiatrist. But it is not always possible to choose; in some hostage-taking situations the role is thrust upon someone simply because he is in the right place at the right time, and he has to do the job as best he can. At other times, however, there is a certain latitude of choice, and both the terrorist and the beleaguered authorities may have a voice in selecting the person on whose offices their fates will rest. Perhaps surprisingly, both will have certain interests in common in this endeavor. Both will probably consider it undesirable to have a negotiator who has decision-making authority on behalf of the government—the terrorists for the obvious reason that such a person will probably be almost cripplingly biased, the government because such a person is likely to act hastily and may commit the authorities, in the interests of a pacific outcome, to an unpalatable or unacceptable course of action.

Both sides will usually agree, then, that the negotiator should be, in effect, a pawn, with little autonomy in the area of policy. That doesn't mean he should not be able to think quickly and act decisively if the occasion requires it, but the necessity of checking major steps with higher-up authorities gives both sides time to think, and prevents impulsive reactions. In addition the negotiator should be an essentially sympathetic individual in whom both sides can have confidence. He must be able to speak the terrorists' language. On a literal as well as a psychological level this is not a trivial requirement. International travel being what it is, it is not unusual to find terrorists and their victims cooped up in a railroad car or an airplane cabin in a country where no one can understand what they are saying. Agonizing delays can be created while someone with the right linguistic abilities is sought, and if negotiation must proceed through a thicket of half-understood phrases there are all too many opportunities for a deadly mistake.

It should go without saying that the negotiator must be willing and able to stand up to prolonged stress. He * will be at the center of a tension-filled activity that could last for days. Throughout this whole time he must remain calm, articulate, observant, and rational, able to present each side's arguments effectively to the other with an understanding of the policy and security issues at stake on both sides. He must be able to see and to weigh alternatives, even though he will not be the one to decide finally which one is chosen. For all these reasons a hostage makes a poor negotiator and should not be used. As a negotiator a hostage has three blatant flaws: he will do almost anything to ease the painful pressure on himself as soon as possible; he is in a close emotional relationship with the terrorist, whom he sees paradoxically as having his welfare at heart much more sincerely than the authorities do; and he is, owing to his situation, incapable of seeing objectively the range of alternative solutions to the problem created

* Some police forces object to using women as primary negotiators, ostensibly on the ground that male hostage takers will feel sexually threatened and female hostage takers will feel jealous.

by his capture. The pilot of a hijacked airplane, therefore, often makes a very bad negotiator, though he may often be thrust into the position because he is in contact from the beginning with both the authorities on the ground and the terrorists in the air. Captain Carey's shaky voice coming over the radio during the 1976 TWA hijacking by Croatian nationalists was strong proof that almost anyone else should have been chosen to negotiate with the terrorists. And the fascinating telephone dialogue between Swedish bank hostage Kristin Ehnmark and Prime Minister Olof Palme during Jan Olsson's attempt to bargain his way to freedom clearly shows the uselessness of the hostage as negotiator:

"I want you to let us go away with the robber. Give them the foreign currency and two guns and let us drive off."

"But one can't do that. Consider the situation: they were robbing a bank and shooting at the police." . . .

"But, darling Olof, don't you understand that we are starting to feel the pressure here—all of us? I want to come out with these two guys. . . ."

"Then the risks would be greater for you." . . .

"But, dearest Olof, sweetheart, it may sound stupid, but I want to go with the two [Olsson and his friend Clark]."

"Why?"

"Because I trust them. I know they would let us go as long as the police don't chase us." . . .

"Why do you suppose the police have not attacked?"

"I don't know."

"Don't you understand that it is out of consideration for you? . . . I can hear someone prompting you."

"No, there's no one behind my back. . . . Why can't you make me Prime Minister for this evening?"

A good negotiator will have both an external strategy vis-à-vis the hostage taker and the authorities, and a set of internal guideposts, questions, tactics, and artifices. "There are certain invariables," says Frank Bolz. "You do not give them weapons. You do not exchange prisoners. You never exchange a police officer for a hostage, because that would put the negotiations on a subjective basis." It is useless to pretend the negotiator doesn't take sides. He is almost always on the side of the hostages, and this natural bias shapes his external strategy. His aim is to prolong the hostage-taking episode, not indefinitely, but long enough for several important things to happen. First, both sides, the terrorists and the authorities, must have time to adjust to the shocking realignment of forces that a kidnapping or hijacking entails. They must get past the stage of panic when either side could pull a trigger on any provocation at all. Second, enough time must pass to allow the kidnapper and his captive to become "friends." The closer that relationship becomes, the harder it will be for the kidnapper to shoot his victim, and the harder *that* is, the less likely he will be to carry out threats if his steep demands are not met. Recognizing this, he may in fact voluntarily scale down some of his demands. Third, the longer a hostage-taking episode goes on, the more uncomfortable both the kidnappers and their victims become. This is particularly true when their location is known by the authorities and they have no freedom of movement.

Both the skill of negotiators and the patience of police were tested dramatically in the spring of 1977 when gunmen seized hostages almost simultaneously in three buildings in downtown Washington, D.C. Just after eleven A.M. on March 9, a U-Haul van pulled up next to the B'nai B'rith headquarters on Rhode Island Avenue and disgorged seven men clad in jeans and carrying guitar cases. Rushing into the lobby of the building, they produced rifles, shotguns, and a crossbow. As an elevator full of passengers opened on the ground floor, one of the gunmen yelled, "Get down or we'll blow your heads off!" Slashing a machete at every imagined resistance, firing their guns on any provocation, they advanced on the terrified people. "They killed my babies and shot my women!" screamed the leader, Hamaas Abdul Khaalis, a fifty-six-year-old Hanafi Muslim, referring to a Black Muslim attack four years earlier that killed five of his children. "Now they will listen to us—or heads will roll."

Within three hours other contingents of the Hanafi Muslims

secured hostages in two more sites: the Islamic Center near Rock Creek Park and the city hall (called the District Building) on Fourteenth Street. At the third location the Muslims blasted a shotgun in the chest of Maurice Williams, a young radio reporter, and he died in a pool of blood. The Hanafis were now in full control of all three buildings.

From his headquarters in the B'nai B'rith building Khaalis issued demands that a current motion picture, *Mohammed, Messenger of God*, be removed instantly from theaters around the country, that the imprisoned killers of his children be brought to him, and that police return a $750 fine leveled against him four years earlier for contempt of court during the trial of his children's killers. It was apparent that the most dangerous demand was the second one, for Khaalis evidently wanted to settle a blood score. He also told a reporter to get in touch with Secretary of State Cyrus Vance and the ambassadors of Muslim countries: "We are going to kill foreign Muslims at the Islamic Center [and] create an international incident." In this event the political motives were secondary to the personal, but the negotiating task nevertheless in many ways resembled that arising from a political terrorist incident.

Police were rushed in to all three sites, under the overall direction of Chief Maurice Cullinane, a man well versed in the art and theory of hostage negotiation. The State Department began searching for sympathetic persons in the Islamic diplomatic community. The White House held hasty staff conferences, which were dominated by the fear that Khaalis would ask President Carter to speak with him, as Carter had done only a week or so earlier with Cleveland hostage taker Cory C. Moore. Staff members concluded it was important for the president to keep the lowest possible profile throughout these negotiations and that only if absolutely necessary would Carter talk with Khaalis—and then only after all hostages were released.

Meanwhile, while the Hanafi Muslims brandished shotguns over the prostrate figures of their hostages, bound hand and foot and lying face down on the floor, the diplomatic community responded to the emergency. Ambassador Ashraf

Ghorbal of Egypt volunteered to help in the negotiations, then secured the services of Ambassador Sahabzada Yaqub-Khan of Pakistan. Their first call to Khaalis was disappointing. Khaalis ranted for a long time—a catalogue of grievances that served to air his frustrations and hostility without making him visibly calmer. When the ambassadors tried quoting scripture to him he retorted, "Don't teach me the Koran. I know the Koran better than you."

Later they were joined by Ambassador Ardeshir Zahedi of Iran, who had flown in from Paris. After further discussions with Cullinane over roast beef sandwiches and coffee they tried out a new text on Khaalis: "Let not the hatred of some people in once shutting you out of the sacred mosque lead you to transgression. . . . Fear Allah, for Allah is strict in punishment." Khaalis, however, matched them verse for verse with texts on the doctrine of divine retribution. The ambassadors were duly impressed but not defeated.

All night they tried this routine, alternating phone calls for persuasion and "letting off steam" with periods of silence when Khaalis had no contact with the outside world. But Khaalis remained adamant. Twelve more hours passed. Finally, at five-thirty P.M. the following day he phoned out to the negotiating team, asking for a face-to-face meeting with Yaqub-Khan. The problem was logistical. When Cullinane suggested he come down unarmed to the lobby of the B'nai B'rith building, he replied, "I'll be damned if I'm going to come down and be shot by your people." At last it was agreed that all three ambassadors, plus Cullinane and an assistant, would meet with Khaalis and his son-in-law Aziz. A table and chairs were set up in the lobby and Khaalis, unarmed, descended the elevator in which more than thirty hours earlier he and his henchmen had startled what were to be the first hostages taken in the excruciating adventure. He greeted the ambassadors in Arabic, ritually hugging each one three times. Then, in English, he exchanged verses from the Koran with them.

After much discussion, Ghorbal suggested that Khaalis release thirty hostages as a gesture of good faith. It was plain that the terrorist needed a way to end the episode gracefully and save face. He chose this opening. Looking around the table, he simply offered to release them all.

His only condition had to do with saving face rather than settling old scores or even saving his own skin: he wanted to "put his house in order" before facing indictments and jail. After studying his psychological profile, police officials decided he was a safe risk. He was allowed to return home on the understanding that he would first appear before a judge to be granted release on his own recognizance and later would appear for a court hearing on charges of armed kidnapping. He must surrender his passport and all firearms. Before his court appearance he would be under virtual house arrest. Khaalis agreed to these provisions. He ordered his comrades in the other buildings to surrender, which they did within minutes. Then he was escorted away by the police. At 5:10 the next morning, he appeared at a special court session, then, freed from handcuffs, walked out the door between two guards, wearing a trenchcoat and cap, puffing a long cigar.

It was a victory for the strategy of patient negotiation, and a theatrical triumph for the Islamic ambassadors. Each of them a striking figure in his own right, together they had done much to convince Americans that they (and by extension the countries they represented) were decent, law-abiding, and religious; sympathetic, intelligent, persistent, and ingenious. One of the side benefits of the publicity accompanying a terrorist episode is that a good negotiator can look very good indeed.

There are other advantages to patience and persistence in such situations. Prolonging negotiations can make it possible for police to locate the hostage takers' hideout and thus, as we have seen, suddenly change the terms of the negotiations. This is exactly what happened in the fall of 1970 when separatist terrorists from the Front de Liberation du Quebec (FLQ) in Montreal kidnapped James Cross, a senior British trade commissioner in Quebec, and demanded $500,000 and the release of twenty-three political prisoners (fellow separatists) in exchange for his safe return. When the government of Prime Minister Pierre Trudeau refused even to consider the exchange, the terrorist group responded by kidnapping Pierre LaPorte, the Quebec Minister of Labor and Immigration. Still the Trudeau government stood firm, and in fact invoked Canada's War Measures Act, permitting it to round up suspects at will and detain them without trial. One day later, on October 17, the separatists announced: "Pierre LaPorte, Minister of Unemployment and Assimilation, was executed at 6:18 tonight by the Dieppe Cell (Royal 22nd); we shall conquer. FLQ." Shortly after that LaPorte's body was found wrapped in bloody blankets and stuffed in the trunk of a taxi in downtown Montreal. He had been strangled with a fine chain holding a religious medal, apparently after an unsuccessful attempt to escape through a window.

Rather than capitulate, the Trudeau government continued its separatist roundup. From his secret place of captivity Cross sent a letter begging the Royal Canadian Mounted Police not to search out the hideout, for he was sure he would be killed. The RCMP studied the letter for clues but ignored the request. Gradually, however, the clues began to accumulate. Three weeks later, police arrested a student who admitted his involvement in the LaPorte kidnapping but denied that he had participated in the murder. He named three accomplices. The police arrested them too and followed up all the information they spilled during interrogation. On December 2, in the suburban north of the sprawling city, police located an apartment at 10945 Des Recolletts Street where a cell of separatists held James Cross. Quietly they surrounded the three-story building, cordoned off two city blocks around it, and then made contact with the occupants. Cross was still alive.

Immediately the terms of the negotiations were shifted. Cross's life was no longer a lever for the release of twenty-three imprisoned separatists; it would, at best, serve to protect his own captors from arrest and imprisonment. That is what happened. Of the four men involved in the kidnapping, three were present in the apartment when police surrounded it. In a sense they now were hostages of the police even as Cross was their hostage. A little later someone in the apartment tossed a lead pipe out the window. Inside was a note agreeing to negotiations. The exchange was simple: the three terrorists —Marc Carbonneau, Jacques Lanctot, and Pierre Seguin— were flown to Havana, and on their arrival Cuban diplomats in Montreal, who had acted as intermediaries, set James Cross free.

Whether LaPorte's life could have been saved by a minor gesture that would have bought time until police could locate his captors' hideout we can never know; but the policy worked with Cross and, though it did not bag his kidnappers, kept the imprisoned terrorists in the government's hands and added other violent separatists to their number besides.

Once the hostage holder's location is known, the more restricted his surroundings, the more desperate his situation. An airplane in flight must land after only a few hours aloft. And even if it lands in a country friendly to the hijackers, it is vulnerable to sabotage that can prevent it from taking off again. From this point the plight of the hostage holder can only get worse. The airplane cabin becomes a torture chamber —stifling or frigid depending on the outside temperature, the air stale, the toilets overflowing, the food depleted. Hostages begin to get sick. Sick hostages are bad for the terrorists' morale and bad for their public image. Dead ones are worse for both and, of course, no longer useful as bargaining tokens. It becomes imperative to come to an accommodation of some sort with the negotiators, and time is on their side. Some concessions begin to look like a small price to pay to end the discomfort.

In addition to prolonging the episode, the negotiator will want to convince the hostage takers of the impossibility of realizing all their demands, and the authorities of the necessity of acceding to some of them, or at least of making certain token concessions. His aim is to minimize expectations. In the process he allows each side to think the other is intransigent, that only by the supreme exercise of his persuasive powers can there be even a slight softening of position. In this way the hostage takers may be led to scale down their demands, while the authorities may decide that it is not so great a compromise to the national image after all if, once the captives are released, the hostage takers are given safe conduct to the country of their choice.

In the course of telling the hostage takers how impossibly steep their demands are, the negotiator will try to convince them that their hostages are actually useless to them. Several plausible arguments may be used along the lines of Professor Selten's story. The nation at which the demands are directed may have announced a policy of "no negotiations with terrorists." In such a case a negotiator representing another country may convincingly argue, "Even though you shoot every one of the hostages they will not yield to your demands but will rush to overpower you. You will either be killed on the spot or captured, tried, and probably executed." Or the negotiator may argue, "Even if some of your demands are met, the authorities will not let you take the hostages with you to guarantee safe conduct. Once you have released them you are vulnerable and will doubtless be caught. We'll make a fair trade: we'll concede your main demands; in return you release the hostages and give yourselves up." This argument is effective in some terrorist hostage-holding situations, but not in others, where the terrorist thinks he has a reasonable chance of escaping capture, either because the negotiator is bluffing about the government's firmness or because alternate escape routes are available. The negotiator's third argument is of use only in the case of airplane hijacking, and then only when he is reasonably sure that the hijackers do not want to die. He can point out to them that any major violence while the plane is aloft is likely to destroy it and everyone aboard; realistically, it makes little sense to point a gun at the pilot's head, since to shoot him is to commit suicide as well. And if the pilot is not personally threatened he may land where and when he likes. Once the plane is on the ground everyone aboard, terrorists included, is in a tight spot. To shoot a hostage would cause police agents to rush the plane and overpower the hijackers. The hijacker has put himself in a ticklish position: Only if he is obviously willing to die *along with his hostages* can he pose a convincing threat.

Every good negotiator knows that in the course of protracted negotiations there comes one psychological moment when the most powerful argument can be made to the most telling effect. If it is made too early in the proceedings its force may be lost, since the parties will not feel themselves in sufficiently dire straits to give it serious attention, and then the talks will be deadlocked. On the other hand, if the negotiator waits too long, frayed nerves or desperation may lead the authorities to an ill-advised attack or the terrorists to a frantic move that could kill several hostages. When the right point comes, some concession must usually be made to the hostage takers, but it may be more apparent than real. That point came for the Croatian hijackers of the TWA jetliner in 1976 when the plane was on the ground at Charles de Gaulle Airport in Paris, having come there from New York by way of Montreal; Gander, Newfoundland; and Shannon, Ireland. Earlier we witnessed this event from the viewpoint of the hijackers. Now consider the role and perspective of the negotiator. Along the way the plane and its escort (needed for the transatlantic flight) had dropped leaflets announcing the hijackers' case, and newspapers had complied with their demands to publish their elaborate manifestos. They had achieved part of their objective and they had spilled no blood. Negotiators could see that they were tired and worn out, and so were the hostages. Now, with the plane's landing gear disabled by French police and the knowledge that the "bombs" tied around their waists were fakes, they clearly wanted only to negotiate the promise that they would not be prosecuted if they released their hostages.

"Look," said the negotiator who was doing the talking for the French government. "Whatever happens, you're going to get captured. Your plane can't take off. You harm one hostage and the police storm the plane. You make a run for it and the police catch you. If you are caught by the French police you'll be tried in the French courts and very likely convicted and executed. Not a pretty future to look forward to. But if you give yourself up to the American police you'll be tried in the American courts and probably convicted, but you won't be executed. Instead you'll draw a long prison sentence with a chance of eventual parole. You're young still. You have a long life ahead of you. Think it over. We're offering you a real choice. If you surrender to the Americans you'll have made your cause known *and* you'll still be alive to enjoy your success."

They thought it over. They did care. The moment was right and the argument was very attractive. The next moment the group surrendered to the American police.

If every hostage-taking episode were simply a struggle between the terrorists and the authorities—with the negotiator as a medium and with the hostages keeping the stakes of the game high—the problems of successful resolution would be sufficiently complicated, but strategists might have at least a little confidence in their plans, a little hope for a successful outcome. But extraneous forces cannot be kept out of the diagram. One of the strongest and most problematic is the communications media.

The more one considers terrorism as a phenomenon, the less it resembles other forms of violence and the more it looks like a form of communication. There is a "speaker" (the terrorist), an "audience" (the primary victim and all the other onlookers in the world), and a "language" (the threat of violence against an innocent party). There is also—and this is what makes terrorism so successful in our time—a means for transmitting the message to the audience: television, radio, and the newspapers, all with the ability to purvey hostage-taking stories *while they are happening.* As a consequence, the audience of a hostage-taking episode is not limited to those who are not involved; it includes the terrorists themselves. Terrorists watch themselves on television. They read stories about themselves in newspapers. They hear commentators analyze their effects on the authorities and their chances of getting away with their exploits. Small wonder that, like all the rest of us, they are influenced by what they hear. Such communication almost always works in favor of the terrorist, since it tells him things his opponent already knows, without divulging to the opponent any secrets of the terrorist. The Tupamaros who held Daniel Mitrione captive learned from radio and television that some of their band had been arrested by the police and were able to adjust their strategy accordingly. The kidnappers of James Cross learned from the radio that the police were closing in on their hideout and they so unnerved Cross that he wrote to the police begging them to stop. Authorities who have a secret ulterior negotiating position—a concession, say, which they do not wish to make known unless they are driven to the wall—had better make sure their secrets are kept hidden from the press as well, or they will lose any strategic advantage in talks with the terrorists.

In addition, all countries are vulnerable, and democratic countries especially so, to public pressures generated by media coverage of terrorist episodes and brought to bear in the form of demonstrations urging—even demanding—a particular negotiating posture or a particular concession. In this way, as we have seen, Israel was compelled to abandon her announced policy of nonnegotiation with terrorists when the relatives of the Entebbe hijack victims, aroused by the press reports of mounting danger to the captives, stormed the government chambers in Tel Aviv and demanded that negotiations begin at once.

There are, then, three principal ways in which the media can become involved in a terrorist hostage-taking episode. First, they provide immediate reflection of the act and continuous commentary on it while it is going on, thus allowing the hostage takers to assess public and governmental response to their action and adjust their demands and threats accordingly. Second, they constitute a forum for the broadcast of manifestos and demands by the hostage takers, either willingly because these items are newsworthy, or under pressure from the hostage takers, who threaten violence to their captives if their views are not published. Third, they offer (though unintentionally) a powerful defense of the terrorists against charges once the episode is over, for an action attended by such publicity is bound to arouse public passions to such an extent that a fair trial anywhere in the world becomes extremely difficult to bring off.

During the time that SLA members held Patricia Hearst

hostage in a closet of their Berkeley apartment, they kept track of the attempts by the outside world to track them down. Radio station KPFA, used as a communications point by the SLA, who left tapes of Patty's voice there for transmittal to her family and the world at large, was also a source of news on the futile efforts of police to locate the hideout. The *San Francisco Examiner*, the newspaper owned by Patty's father, almost daily provided semiofficial statements on the current negotiating posture of the family. Mrs. Hearst appeared on television first to plead with the hostage takers to release Patty, later to plead with her daughter to return to the family and the life she had so dramatically renounced after joining her captors. SLA members watched not only these moments on television, but also the straight news reports describing the search for the hideout. Once Patty was "converted," movement was easier; it became possible to stay one or more jumps ahead of police and the FBI simply by watching the television reports of their search.

The argument that in the public interest the media should refrain from reporting sensitive information about hostage-taking events is stoutly resisted by editors, reporters, and newspaper and broadcasting executives. They point out that if such information is detrimental to the goals of the police or the FBI, then it is the duty of those agencies to keep their movements and plans secret, even from the press. They frequently neglect to recall that the press uses every means ingenuity can suggest to uncover secrets from every available source, even to the point of invoking (so far unsuccessfully) the federal Freedom of Information Act to compel the disclosure of personal information held by government administrative agencies. On the other hand, during times perceived *by the media* as involving serious national crisis, editors and program directors have cooperated with government censorship of military information or, in the case of the Vietnam War, have imposed an effective self-censorship that lasted until late in the sixties when the tide of public opinion began to turn against the war and it became politically safer to defy the official desire for a loyal press in favor of a growing unofficial clamor for the truth about the conduct of the war. Only then was the time ripe to publish the ugly story of My Lai.

On the question of "demand publishing" of terrorists' manifestos, newspapers evince a certain ambivalence. In countries with strong traditions of a free press, any loss of editorial control over what goes into the paper and what does not is viewed with suspicion and alarm; editors would tend to reject on principle the requirement that they publish someone's political rantings. On the other hand a newspaper that refuses to publish a manifesto in accordance with, say, an airplane hijacker's demands runs the risk of seeing an entire plane blown up and all passengers killed on account of its policies. Such an event, to put it crassly, would be bad for circulation.

Fortunately (for the papers), the writings of terrorists, whether they are rational or irrational, angry or visionary, often make good copy. People appear at least as interested in learning the grievances of Croatian nationalists, especially when they have hijacked a plane that is even now on its circuitous way to Paris, as they are in the president's State of the Union address. That a newspaper in publishing such a document is cooperating in the purpose of the terrorist effort and thereby encouraging other actions like it seems to be of less concern, in the long run, than the simultaneous fulfillment of the hijackers' demands for public attention (thereby perhaps saving the captives from death) and the public's newly whetted thirst for information about the motives behind a dramatic exploit.

On February 27, 1975, members of the Baader-Meinhof gang kidnapped German politician Peter Lorenz and demanded in exchange for his life the release of five of their imprisoned comrades. Negotiations were protracted over three days, but in the end everything went like clockwork: the terrorists were set free, given $10,000 each, and flown first class by Lufthansa to the Middle East. Throughout the episode the networks experienced a certain guilty pleasure. One television editor commented, "For 72 hours we just lost control of the medium. We shifted shows to meet their timetable. Our cameras had to be in position to record each of the prisoners as they boarded the plane, and our news coverage had to include prepared statements at their dictation. There is plenty of underworld crime on our screens, but up until now Kojak and Columbo were always in charge. Now it was the real thing, and it was the gangsters who wrote the scripts and programmed the mass media." Yet, during those three days, tens of millions of Germans were glued to their television sets. In fact, the most consistently successful terrorist ploy has been the drive to seize public attention. In this drive the media have cooperated unstintingly. That, after all, is their function.

So far we have treated the hostages as a passive quantity in the constellation of forces that affect the outcome of a hostage-taking enterprise; but of course they are anything but passive, and in fact their effect can be decisive. In the chapter on the psychology of terrorism we saw a drunken passenger nearly cause the explosion of a grenade in a hijacked airplane. Near the end of the excruciating Entebbe hijacking episode a conversation (recounted earlier) between one of the terrorists and a former inmate of a Nazi concentration camp prepared for a denouement in which the terrorist chose to face the fire of the invading Israeli commandos but would not turn his machine gun on his captives. Hostages can attack their captors, they can passively resist them, they can become friends with them, or they can even decide to join them, as Patty Hearst joined the Symbionese Liberation Army. Simply in terms of survival, and leaving all other moral issues aside, the last two alternatives are immeasurably preferable to the first two. Attacking a terrorist who has just taken you hostage is a very good way to die quickly. Resisting him by refusing to cooperate or to talk with him will not ingratiate you with him, and may, therefore, have the unfortunate consequence of making it easier for him to shoot you if negotiations don't work out to his liking. "If you're ever taken hostage and you are hooded or blindfolded or put into a closet, your chances of coming out alive are practically nil," says one psychiatrist.

He was thinking mainly of the mentally disturbed hostage taker, but the problem is only slightly less terrifying for the victims of political terrorists.

Death at the hands of kidnappers is an occupational hazard for ambassadors and other officials who are so firmly committed to an opposing ideology, and so well trained in the decorum of the government or corporate representative, that they actually endanger their own survival. During the period from 1968 to 1975, at least seven senior United States diplomats were kidnapped, and four of these, at the level of ambassador or chief of mission, were killed. Clearly their survival rate was much lower than that for other hostages, though the reasons are complex. To kill an ambassador is a sharper blow at another country than the killing of an ordinary citizen would be, and terrorists are often tempted to make use of this more powerful weapon. It may also be true—as many worried foreign service officers in the U.S. State Department think— that some governments are less reluctant to sacrifice a diplomat than a private citizen. After all, the diplomat has accepted a fairly high degree of risk in agreeing to represent his country in places where it (and he) may well be unpopular, whereas the private citizen depends on his government for protection from just such risks.

But clearly the best policy, assuming you don't really have a change of heart and join your captors, is to be as easy to get along with as possible. It worked for Eric Leupin. On January 31, 1975, the Canadian-born Honorary Dutch Consul was kidnapped from his farm in Colombia by terrorists from the Revolutionary Armed Forces, who demanded $1 million from the Dutch government, $30,000 from his family, and the release of three political prisoners. The Dutch government refused to respond to the demand; the diplomat's family declined comment to the press. For the indefinite future after that day in January, Leupin was on his own. He soon realized that, as he said, his captors were ruthless and would stop at nothing to achieve their goals. "I am an optimist," Leupin said later. "I never thought of committing suicide, but the mental agony was terrible: the uncertainty of not knowing what was going to happen to me." Weeks dragged on and turned into months. He became increasingly friendly with his captors, who had taken him to a hideaway in the Andes Mountains. And although they guarded him day and night, he appreciated their fair treatment of him and the ample food and clothing they provided. Had he been there by choice, he might have enjoyed it: the terrorists fed him game, trout, corn, rice, and potatoes. Nevertheless, he tried to escape one day after he had been imprisoned for several months. "But you can't walk in the jungles, and they recaptured me," he said. "They weren't mad at me."

"We know it's your duty to try to escape," his captors told him, "but from now on we're going to guard you so well that you won't have another chance."

More months went by. Finally, twenty months after he had first been captured, Leupin's captors walked him through the mountains for nine days, handed him ten dollars, and set him free. He had to wait twelve hours before a taxi appeared. He took it to the home of a friend and paid the driver with the terrorists' ten dollars.

Few kidnappings last so long, and few finally end so well. Terrorists start out angry, and they provoke anger in their primary victims. Under such conditions both sides find compromise difficult and sometimes impossible. Yet a successful outcome nearly always depends on compromise. "Successful" here means, of course, an outcome in which nobody is killed. This is the bystander's definition of success. For Israel the outcome of the Entebbe hijacking was successful because the hostages were rescued, even though all the terrorists and many Ugandan guards were killed in the process. For the Black September group, the Munich episode was at least a partial success, even though eleven Israeli athletes lost their lives and the terrorists themselves were arrested and jailed (only to be released weeks later by means of another hijacking exploit). A strong political bias will correspondingly bias the preference as to outcome, just as it often determines who is called a terrorist in the first place. No one can argue with a strong political bias that is acknowledged as such. But enough evidence has already been reviewed to convince the careful and the judicious that the defeat of terrorist expectations on a particular occasion, or even the killing or arrest of hostage takers, cannot dilute the long-term threat.

In plain terms, it is no victory over terrorism to kill the terrorists responsible for a particular episode. Placed by a terrorist in a concede-or-else situation, the rational primary victim will attempt to cut his losses in the short term and, in the long term, neutralize the cause of the unrest expressed through such violence. At the moment when the gun is pointed at someone's head or the grenade with the safety pin out is brandished about the aircraft in flight, there is no time to worry about the long term. The job at hand is to make sure that no one gets killed.

One way to do this, of course, would be to give the terrorist everything he wanted. When the hostage's value to the primary victim is very high (and it must be acknowledged that the value placed on a life will vary depending on whom the life belongs to), the tendency is to avoid negotiating, even to fear it, and to cooperate fully with only the end of recovery in view. From one point of view this is a safe policy, but it is also expensive. It must be remembered that the hostage taker has placed himself in a very risky situation too, and, though he will not say so, he is negotiating for his own life as well as for the concessions he had demanded. As the bank manager described in an earlier chapter found out to his wife's chagrin, there is often a lot of leeway between a hostage taker's top price and the price he is willing to accept.

Another approach is to lie. Promise the terrorist anything, but have no qualms about reneging once the hostage is returned. Pretend concessions are just around the corner when really you have no intention of making them, and thus protract negotiations until the hostage takers are tired or psychologically unable to harm their captives. Terrorists like other people may indulge themselves in a certain amount of hope— in this case that the harrowing adventure they have embarked on will somehow end safely and with no loss of face. They may therefore be willing to wait longer than cold-blooded reason would dictate for some concrete concession.

This approach has occasionally been tried with nonpolitical hostage takers and has succeeded. Early in 1977 Anthony Kiritsis walked into the offices of the Indiana mortgage company that had recently foreclosed on his $130,000 loan. He calmly pointed a sawed-off shotgun at the head of Richard Hall, a member of the family that owns the company, and wired the gun barrel to Hall's neck, with a "dead man" wire running from the trigger to his own head, so that if someone shot him, his gun would still go off, killing Hall. Escorting Hall to a nearby police car, he commanded the startled driver to drive back to his apartment, where for the next sixty-three hours he kept police at bay with his shotgun at Hall's head, an announcement that the apartment was mined with a hundred pounds of dynamite, and three demands: he wanted all mention of his mortgage to be expunged from company records, he wanted an apology from the company for the foreclosure, and he wanted a guarantee of immunity from all prosecution once Hall was released. The first two demands were directed at the mortgage company, and Hall's family unhesitatingly gave in to them. The third was directed at the federal and state law enforcement officials who, along with the police, were massed a safe distance across from the apartment. For a time they demurred, then they agreed to the terms. By this time the episode had gone on for over two days. Both kidnapper and hostage had slept fitfully and very briefly. Kiritsis realized he couldn't hold out forever. Night was falling for the third time since the episode began and he was claustrophobic. Hostage taking was turning out to have its difficulties. He was disposed to accept the offer, and at eleven P.M. he did.

As soon as he let Hall go the police rushed him, collared him, and booked him for the very crimes he thought he had bargained his way out of. "This is a cheap-ass shot!" were the last words reporters heard him say as the guards led him away.

In this case a lie worked. It prevented bloodshed and resulted in the apprehension of the kidnapper. It is only prudent to add, however, that later would-be kidnappers would probably be smarter, having learned from Kiritsis' experience, and would demand not an easily broken promise of immunity but transportation out of the country, with the hostage in tow, to a nation lacking an extradition treaty with the United States or disposed to treat terrorists kindly for historical or ideological reasons. The hostage could always be sent back safely once the hostage taker's life and liberty were no longer in danger.

Most political terrorists would not have fallen for a mere promise in the first place. The experienced and the desperate may be willing to pull the trigger at an early stage in the proceedings, thus demonstrating that they mean business and often incidentally aiding their cause by enlisting the frantic relatives of the survivors in concerted pressure to force the government toward a more conciliatory position. Tricks therefore are tricky. They may work if the hostage holders are nervous and inexperienced and hopeful, if they lack discipline among themselves, or if they appear to have no carefully worked out schedule of demands. They may not work if these conditions do not obtain. The problem is that conditions of this sort are not easy to judge. The hostage taker's resources are sometimes known only imperfectly. Does he really have weapons? Bombs? How many people are in his party and what are they capable of? Are there other terrorists nearby who might come to offer aid?

A second problem of such trickery is that it invites retaliation. While it may succeed in resolving the immediate problem of disarming the kidnappers and freeing the hostages, it often provokes a further terrorist exploit designed at once to vent anger by getting revenge, to secure release of terrorists captured during the earlier exploit, and to demonstrate to the world at large that the terrorists can stand up to their oppressors. Law enforcement officials and government policy makers who persist in thinking of political hostage taking in the terms suggested by the film *Dog Day Afternoon* would be well advised to ponder the differences. In that film—based on a real incident—two robbers, acting on their own, capture and hold several members of the staff in the course of robbing a New York City bank. After a prolonged siege they are lured out of the bank, with hostages in tow, to a van driven by an FBI officer which will ostensibly take them to a plane that will fly them to neutral territory (envisioned by the robbers as either another country or Wyoming). Arriving at the airport, the robber riding "shotgun" is duped into momentarily taking his rifle off the driver, and the driver, grabbing a concealed pistol, shoots him through the forehead at point-blank range. His partner is overpowered, arrested, tried, and jailed. End of story.

Even if most political terrorists were sufficiently stupid, naïve, or unwary to fall for such a ploy, which is possible but but unlikely, the incident would not end there. It is never safe to regard a genuine act of political terrorism as an isolated incident that can be effectively dealt with by criminal justice methods alone. A terrorist in jail is not an incapacitated bandit; he is (to his comrades) a prisoner of war in a long struggle which may see heavy sacrifices on both sides. He can be recaptured. If he is executed, his murder (so it is seen) can be avenged. New troops will be thrown into the sporadic, vicious underground battle. New exploits will be planned.

Prudence, then, dictates that under some conditions it is safer to make concessions. There are no universally accepted guidelines on what to concede; every case is different. But there are commonsense rules about format. Assuming the primary victim is able to choose a negotiator who is sympathetic to his perspective—not a difficult problem, since the hostage taker controls very little outside his own narrowly circumscribed world—the negotiator's aim will be to concede as little as possible and to draw out the negotiating time as long as possible. On the other side, the relatives and friends of the hostage may find the wait almost unendurable, but the longer they can hold out *while keeping negotiations alive*, the better their ultimate chances of success.

But keeping negotiations alive is critical. If they fizzle out, if the hostage takers become convinced that no concessions of any sort are forthcoming, then they may begin carrying out their threats. On March 1, 1973, Palestinian guerrillas of the Black September movement kidnapped Cleo Noel, the United

States ambassador to the Sudan, along with George Moore, his deputy chief of mission, Guy Eid, the Belgian chargé d'affaires, and Jordanian and Saudi Arabian diplomats. In response to demands for the release of Arab political prisoners in several countries, including Abu Daoud in Amman, Jordan, and Sirhan Sirhan in America, the United States government reiterated its hard-line position: no negotiations with terrorists. In this it was echoed by Israel and Jordan. (In fact, the American government was shortly to fly "observer" William Macomber of the State Department to Khartoum, Sudan, where the prisoners were being held in the Saudi Arabian embassy, but the Palestinians did not know this.) Meanwhile, Sudanese troops surrounded the embassy. Angry that their demands were ignored, and desperate to be taken seriously, in the middle of the night during a blinding sandstorm the terrorists shot and killed both Americans and the Belgian. But those were their high cards; now their only hope of saving their own lives was to surrender. Three days later negotiators recognized the strain in their voices over the telephone, sometimes near the breaking point. The Sudanese government offered assurances the terrorists would not be executed, provided they agreed to surrender. That did it. Emerging from the embassy, they flashed a wan victory sign at onlookers and the press, then gave themselves up to the waiting police officers. The Arab diplomats walked out unharmed. It was a "successful" outcome only for those who believe the hard line works and is more important than the lives of diplomats. But from the standpoint of the uncommitted bystander interested only in preserving lives, the entire episode was a disaster. The terrorists did not really want Noel dead, they simply wanted the release of as many imprisoned Arabs as they could bargain for. But they were driven by the apparently intransigent position of their primary victims, and by fears that Sudanese troops might attack during the storm, to overstep themselves in order to prove a point. Both sides lost in that episode.

Apart from the questionable legality of spectacular rescues of the kind Israel pulled off at the Entebbe airport, and the atrocity of massacres used by terrorists in an often futile attempt to buy freedom, as in the case of the shootings at Ma'alot or the Munich Olympics, extreme tactics by either side tend to exacerbate tensions and to invite retaliation. Each "victory" over terrorism, and each "successful" terrorist raid, must therefore be qualified by the further terrorist exploits that follow it. While it is impossible to predict the outcome of any hostage-taking episode by tested rules, certain negotiating stances have proved more consistently successful than others. Negotiators who are trusted (as much as possible) by both sides, and yet are without major decision-making power, are most often successful when they can wrest small concessions from each side, can protract the negotiations until things become uncomfortable for the terrorists, without at the same time allowing either side to conclude that the talks have reached a stalemate, and can convince each side that it has been sufficiently tough not to lose face. Success, let us repeat, means the saving of lives, not the obliteration of the terrorist. Like an army, a terrorist gang operates in a dehumanized mode, making atrocity the stuff of daily life. What the gang members do is appalling and should be stopped, but at the same time they must be listened to; they have something to say.

V

THE GRAND
STRATEGIES
OF TERROR

BUT HOW DOES IT WORK? SINCE TERRORISM IS PRIMARILY
a weapon of the dispossessed, it is all too easy for the frightened majority to assume that simple depravity motivates the
shootings, bombings, and hijackings that lend lurid interest
to the morning newspaper. After all, goes the argument, life
is cheap for the Arabs; blacks are uncivilized and will kill
whites—or each other—at the least opportunity; the Irish are
a nation of drunkards and brawlers. That there could be a
rationale behind terrorism, and, moreover, one that many
people might find attractive if conditions were right, seems
vaguely subversive and not quite credible. But there is a
rationale, and though it would be too much to claim it is
understood by every terrorist who takes up arms against an
unequal opponent, it is rooted in commonly perceived realities, specifically in the relationship of government to the
governed.

Primitively, a government is an organization designed to
protect those who subscribe to it, and to assist them in ac-
quiring basic needs. To do this, it must be at least minimally
responsive to the expression of those needs. It protects by
means of police forces, military forces, and the presumed
safety of numbers. It allows its citizens whatever freedom
of movement and expression they have because it does not
need to protect them individually and constantly, and it does
so to the extent that its leaders perceive it to be unthreatened
by this freedom among its citizens.

A citizen whose life or safety is threatened thus poses a
challenge to his government, for it is the job of government

to offer a credible defense against that threat. To this end governments make and enforce traffic regulations, maintain military defense forces, and refine the methods and equipment of their police. Since police departments have a sharply limited ability to predict and thus forestall crimes, a rising level of crime poses a threat to civil order in the locality where it occurs, by undermining people's confidence in their government's ability to protect them. At such times "law and order" policies and "safe streets" bills are popular, even if they involve certain infringements on civil liberties, because they evidence a government's readiness to deploy its considerable forces for the protection of its constituents.

It is not the aim of most criminals, however, to bring down governments, and therefore there is rarely a systematic attempt by lawbreakers—organized or unorganized—to undermine public confidence in the police (though sometimes clearly this is the effect of their actions). In fact, organized crime profits by the general society's adherence to a structure of laws that, for example, drives up prices for heroin, bookmaking, or prostitution, making them the source of more profitable enterprises than would be possible if they were legal. Moreover, the motive of the professional criminal is usually not terror but profit, and thus while surprise is often necessary if he is to pull off a job successfully, it is a surprise that is likely to dismay the immediate victim rather than frighten his neighbor out of his wits. You come home to find your house ransacked; you call the police, they come and take fingerprints, and you collect on your insurance. The proprietor of the corner cigar store is told at gunpoint to keep quiet and he won't get hurt: he hands over the money, the robber flees, and it's all over; or he resists and gets a bullet in the stomach. Down the street, no one notices. Even the victims of real violence are often not surprised by it; they are beaten by relatives, shot by lovers in the heat of quarrels, or murdered by panicky robbers. At times a criminal creates genuine terror—the rapist in the park or the bank robber who holds several customers hostage—but police methods, designed to show the public that something is being done to solve crimes, offer reassurance if not always protection, and usually succeed in keeping random violence within socially tolerable bounds.

But when the methods associated with ordinary criminals are turned not toward profit or the ventilation of private anger but toward publicity and shock value, a great deal can be done with small resources to depress morale and undermine the faith of the citizens in their government. The reasons are numerous and complex, but the most obvious is that even a powerful government cannot have its forces, police or the military, everywhere at once, so in ordinary circumstances persons who hear of spectacular violent crimes affecting innocent parties will fear for their own lives and those of their families. Should a government bring its full weight to bear in a campaign against terrorist attacks, it must inevitably overcompensate, restricting the personal liberties of many innocent persons for the sake of possibly squelching opportunities for the few among them who are genuine terrorists. It must do this because virtually all citizens will be frightened and will demand protection. On the other hand, a significant number will likely object to restrictions on personal rights that inevitably follow if police, for example, begin arresting suspects without warrant, detaining them without trial, and keeping track of everyone's movements from one city to another.

So governments are caught in a double bind: either fail to increase protection and lose the loyalty of the frightened, or overprotect and risk losing the support of libertarians. There are refinements as well. It may not be enough for the terrorist simply to provoke overreaction by the authorities. Many a hopeful revolutionary has found to his dismay that people did not rise up in revolt against a government that responded with a heavy hand to a minor terrorist episode. "As Guevara had found among the peasants of Bolivia," Gerald McKnight avers, "ordinary men are slow to support bloody revolution." The Baader-Meinhof group in West Germany found this out with some chagrin. By creating a good deal of localized havoc, the group managed to grab headlines in Europe during much of the 1970's, and it successfully exported violence to the Arab countries and Africa. But in spite of financial assistance from the Russians (to aid in publishing the revolutionary journal *Konkret*), it has yet to topple a government or create the state of continuous revolution that is its avowed aim. It has succeeded only in provoking an anxious conservative reaction in West German society.

Similarly, by means of its double kidnapping in 1970 the FLQ in Canada succeeded in provoking the Ottawa government of Pierre Elliot Trudeau to institute the War Measures Act, but it did not succeed in generating any significant public outrage that could be exploited to help melt down the federal structure. On the contrary, most Canadians rallied around Trudeau during the crisis, and the House of Commons voted overwhelmingly to support the War Measures Act.

What is needed, some terrorists have recognized, is a technique for bringing home to the common man the essential injustice, the antipeople attitude, of the government they oppose. Without this, terrorism remains an exercise in negative publicity. Looking back on the time of the Mitrione killing, a former Tupamaro in Uruguay who calls himself "Romeo" confessed, "My sympathy has changed since then. I no longer believe in the guerrilla focus. I feel that the Latin American movements drift away from the path. There is too much violence. I don't believe any more that it gets results." On some occasions at least, even terrorists conclude that strategy works better than violence.

Such strategy may take many forms. A favored technique is to cause the authorities to tip their hand unwittingly, in a way that looks bad, and under maximum publicity. A terrorist venture may do the trick, but sometimes lesser measures will suffice. Ordinary civil disruption succeeded in provoking Chicago police in 1968 into a ludicrous display of force against youths, news reporters, and anyone else in their way, and turned the Democratic National Convention into a public demonstration that the Establishment was paranoid and brutal and hated kids. It cannot be marked as the turning point in public sentiment about the war in Vietnam, nor was it a carefully planned maneuver, but it certainly showed Americans that the guardians of political and legal processes were seriously out of touch with a groundswell of public opinion, especially among the young. In the succeeding months editorials and even political speeches came to take bolder stands against the conduct of domestic and foreign policy—not such a radical stance after all, considering that Lyndon Johnson had, by refusing to seek reelection, effectively admitted failure. A repressive action, provoked perhaps unwittingly by proponents of radical change, became the agent of a slow (some would say token) move toward liberalization in the United States.

All this is a far cry from the revolution that is the aim of most terrorist intriguers, but such revolution is also possible by the same methods; what is required is the massing of public sentiment on the part of the revolutionaries. Paradoxically, well-placed terrorist actions can actually swing public sentiment to the terrorist cause. One of the best examples of this phenomenon occurred in Algeria during the 1950's. At the beginning of the decade Algerian nationalists were confronted by a frustrating political problem: though the French colonial presence in Algeria was noisome to them, most Algerians accepted it without strong objections. The attempts of the anticolonial radicals to rouse public sentiment against the French failed in the face of the claim from Paris that all Algerians were Frenchmen and that there was thus no basis for distinctions or discrimination. A people unaware of its second-class status cannot be brought to revolt against the enforcers of that status. In the case of Algeria, even the identity of the enforcer was ambiguous, since native Algerian police units patrolled the streets of Algiers, and the French presence was dim and fuzzy in most people's minds. The solution, when it finally occurred to the nationalists, was deceptively simple: they began blowing up buses and marketplaces in Algiers.

They anticipated the French response. Paris overreacted in a way typical of threatened governments, but in this case the overreaction was just what the terrorists wanted: suddenly the native Algerian police force disappeared from the streets of Algiers, to be replaced by special forces of grim-faced European Frenchmen, swinging their riot sticks and inspecting people who attempted to board the buses. Now the proof that had been lacking was obvious to every Algerian. In spite of earlier French protestations, Algerians were not considered to be like Frenchmen when it mattered; they were colonials, and when a crisis arose they were not to be trusted—even to police their own people—but were thrust into the background while Frenchmen, the privileged and dominant class, took over. After analyzing those events of the Algerian revolution, the historian David Fromkin concluded that the well-placed terrorist actions of this period, with their carefully calculated consequences, were decisive in marshaling the support of rank-and-file Algerians that eventually led to the nation's independence.

It is quite possible that we are witnessing a similar process in Northern Ireland at the present time, although the colonial dominance of England is more deeply entrenched there. But the predictable reaction from London to each new terrorist outbreak in Belfast—namely the dispatch of more English troops to the very city where they are most hated—has gradually shifted some of the hostility that Catholic and Protestant militants felt toward each other and focused it on the armed foreigner. Whether this shift is profound enough to effect a permanent change in England's relations (never amicable) with the Six Counties, and whether it can end the conditions of civil war that triggered England's military intervention in the first place, remain to be seen, but the latter eventuality seems especially remote.

In sum, the uses of terrorism depend on political conditions at any given moment as well as the conditions the terrorist dissident wishes to bring about. Like the Croatian nationalists, terrorists may simply seek publicity, a means of communicating with the complacent outside world which till that moment had been deaf to their plight. Or like the Palestinian groups they may take hostages in an attempt to force the release of imprisoned comrades or exact specific concessions, such as modified laws or policies affecting a minority group to which the terrorist belongs. Or like the Algerians they may seek to foment a full-blown revolution by disabling and embarrassing the government in power or by causing it to overreact to provocation in a way that alienates the general public and gains wide sympathy for (and promotes active participation in) the terrorists' cause. Finally, like the Japanese United Red Army, they may (somewhat quixotically) try to instigate a worldwide upheaval by committing acts of terror in one country after another, aiming for the final destruction of capitalism or any other system seen as the root of evil in the world.

Which of these policies is actually adopted will be determined largely by the perceived degree of support the government in power has among the people: if popular support is fairly solid and the terrorist contingent comparatively weak, the policy aimed at establishing communication will make the most sense. But if the government's hold over the people is tenuous, and if political inertia is the principal explanation for a failure to revolt, then a well-planned and well-placed terrorist act may cause the government to precipitate its own downfall by taking draconian measures against a perceived terrorist threat and thus breeding popular hostility where before there was only indifference. With this background it is possible to fit terrorism into the context of guerrilla strategy. Any violent man or woman with a grievance may become a terrorist of a sort; the early months of 1977 saw many such self-elected terrorists in the United States, some acting alone, others, like the Hanafi Muslims, working together in a small band. Most of their grievances were personal rather than political or social, and thus most of them fall outside the main focus of our concern. But when the grievances are undeniably political (that is, those of a definable class) and the primary victim is a government, then we are dealing with political terrorism, and often with a good deal of political plotting behind it. When, further, the violent episodes become part of a strategy —a sequence of actions leading toward a certain goal—then the terrorist has become an incipient revolutionary. For his aim at this point is almost never merely to change the government—he has long ago concluded that that cannot be done—but to bring it down.

If his early violent forays are successful the terrorist will often go one step further. He will form his followers into groups with quasi-military programs, and will covertly deploy these groups over the area he wishes to bring under control. Such groups constitute a guerrilla force; they are the first step toward a revolutionary army.

Like a small business just starting out, a small army has a very low chance of survival, and for some of the same reasons: it is inexperienced, its competition is well known and overwhelmingly powerful, its financial resources are limited and its credit poor or nonexistent. Other disadvantages stem from its unique situation as a quasi-military organization: it tends, because of its small numbers and picayune firepower, to be in a poor defensive position. It has trouble taking prisoners, since it has neither the facilities nor the personnel to hold many of them. It cannot return fire for very long without running out of ammunition. Its weapons, often stolen from the opposing army or rounded up hither and yon, are usually old and unreliable; if they break down they cannot easily be replaced.

Poor technology or bad luck can keep the situation desperate. In the waning days of the Mau Mau rebellion, with the loyalist troops hard at their heels, the guerrilla bands in Kenya's Aberdare Mountains made do with pitifully few provisions. Karari Njama describes his attempts to defend his position with the crudest of weapons: "Binihalis offered me his gun with only two bullets, .44 and .375; both could fit in the homemade gun which was a pattern of the manufactured guns. . . . At about two in the afternoon, two Kenya Ng'ombe officers commanding a dozen well-armed African emergency soldiers arrived at the river. . . . I changed my position and standing less than ten yards from them I aimed so that a single bullet could pass through three of them. I then pulled the trigger but failed to release my bullet. I quickly tried a second time with failure. I changed the bullet and by the time I was ready to fire, the first two men had crossed the river and were only seven yards from me and about three yards below me, thus making it impossible for me or them to shoot one another. I pulled my trigger but it failed to discharge." Later, when the enemy was long gone and Njama was trying to explain his frustrating failure to his comrades, the gun unaccountably fired and its recoil knocked him down.

When ammunition became all but unobtainable, Njama tried to discover how gunpowder was made. "I had concluded that it was made of elephants' tusks, charcoal, phosphorus, and some alkali acid. I could see a lot of phosphorus staying as parasites on many decaying logs but I was unable to get acid. My inability to make gunpowder . . . proved to me that we had a lot more to learn from the European's technique."

On the other hand, the smallness of the guerrilla army gives it certain advantages over its opponent which it must exploit to the hilt if it is to survive. For one thing, it often works in native territory: if it is an urban group its members usually know the neighborhood from which they attack. They know every garage and alley; which roofs have fire escapes leading past windows that belong to apartments with concealed back entrances. They have friends who will put them up in a pinch and say nothing. They know that in the back room of a certain ordinary-looking shop they can meet their comrades, regroup, and plan their next move.

Similarly, a rural guerrilla group knows its terrain. It can find its way through forests where the well-equipped pursuers get lost. It knows seasons and weather conditions and can use them to advantage. It can make friends with local people, win their support, use their help in throwing pursuers off the trail. Both urban and rural guerrillas can strike quickly and hide before their enemies can react. Both can make overtures to foreign nations and in this way often win financial assistance, weapons, and even additional troops.

At a certain point in the progress from terrorist organization to revolutionary army the classic techniques of terrorism cease to serve the purpose. No longer dwarfed by its opposition and lacking the attention of the public, the army can begin to abandon the "judo techniques" used by the weak against the strong. Now seemingly random attacks against the innocent no longer have their old value as attention getters; instead they have become a liability since they frighten and alienate the very public whose support is essential to the ultimate success of the movement. As soon as the leaders of the movement cease their attacks against noncombatants and focus their military strength against the army of the entrenched government, they have ceased technically (if not in the minds of their enemies) to be terrorists. Now more threatened than ever by the would-be revolutionaries, the government will intensify its propaganda attacks against them, calling them terrorists and cutthroats. But the *guerrilla* ("little war") may by this time have become an all-out fight for survival.

These are the important distinctions: a guerrilla band is not to be equated with a group of terrorists; it is rather a small organization set up expressly to wage revolutionary war by strike-and-retreat tactics. If in addition it attacks noncombatants or takes them as hostages, it is using terrorist tactics, but as the revolutionary movement grows it will usually abandon these tactics or at least direct them carefully at a group of persons (such as minority whites in Rhodesia) who can be clearly identified with the hated regime.

We have recently seen the Palestine Liberation Organization emerge from a status as a terrorist band and become an internationally respectable spokesman for the displaced Palestinians. The PLO has entered its new role self-consciously; it now looks back with a certain embarrassment on its earlier image as an organization of cold-blooded murderers. That is not to say it wouldn't return to terrorism if conditions demand it, or that it wouldn't (and doesn't) encourage terrorist attacks when necessary by splinter groups that cannot be readily identified with it. But for the time being, in spite of detractors who cannot forget, and others who see an Arab behind almost any terrorist event in the world, the PLO is bent on becoming a respectable nation, even though at the moment it lacks a country.

This air of hard-won respectability is apparent to anyone who visits PLO representatives. Since late 1974 the organization has had a standing invitation to participate as an observer in the work of the United Nations General Assembly. This means its representatives can attend debates and committee hearings and can give speeches, but cannot vote. The status of a "permanent observer" is therefore not quite so grand as that of an ambassador, but it is not trifling either. Accordingly, the New York offices of the permanent observer, Mr. Zehdi Labib Terzi, are on Park Avenue, an apparently respectable and even affluent address. The actual building is rather bleak, however, and a curious visitor ascends the elevator to the seventh floor to emerge in a bare little hallway, uncarpeted, on the other side of which is a closed door with no sign, only a suite number. To the right of the door, in a straight-backed chair, a guard sits negligently, reading a magazine. There is a holstered revolver on his hip. When the visitor explains that he has an appointment with Mr. Terzi he is told to knock at the door.

After a long wait footsteps approach and the door is opened by a young man wearing an open shirt and a mustache. He seems suspicious but tells the visitor to have a seat in a room just off the foyer inside the door; then he disappears. The foyer itself is bare of furniture or carpets. Its only decoration is a series of posters along the walls. Most are in Arabic but a few are in English. Some depict weeping mothers and infants, others show fists clutching rifles. The general theme is "we shall overcome." The waiting room off the foyer is furnished with a plastic-covered sofa and a small table. On the table are pamphlets with titles like *Revolution until Victory*, *Political and Armed Struggle*, and *A Strategy for the Liberation of Palestine*. After a little while another young man, also in shirt-sleeves, appears in the doorway. "Are you here to see Mr. Terzi? This way." He leads the visitor through a series of bare rooms. It is as if the PLO had just moved in, were not sure how long they would be staying, and in any case could not afford (or did not want) bourgeois amenities. At last the visitor comes to a large room with a desk and a secretary. Off to the left is a smaller office that looks as if some care had been spent on it. There is a rug on the floor, plants, a large desk. This is Terzi's office and the visitor is beckoned inside.

Terzi is a short, rotund man with a goatee. He is proud of the PLO's status in the international community and its role as an observer at the United Nations, and he doesn't much like to hear the PLO described as a terrorist organization. The word has a bad sound. What, after all, does it mean? he asks. Violence against noncombatants? Then were the nuclear bombings of Hiroshima and Nagasaki terrorism? Or the fire-bombing of Dresden by Allied forces? Yes, his visitor admits, these were actions of the same type, though the intent was perhaps not quite the same. But surely, says Terzi, such violence by powerful governments and international coalitions is far more lethal, more destructive, more "serious" than that used by the so-called terrorist groups. "And besides," he adds, "how can you say who is and who is not a combatant? We believe, for example, that every citizen of our enemy [Israel] is a potential soldier. If we don't attack them first, they will attack us. They have proved that many times in the past."

"But surely you can't regard even children as potential attackers. Was not the attack at Ma'alot an unwarranted murder of innocents?"

"But remember—who fired the first shots at Ma'alot? It was the Israeli soldiers."

"Still, the children were hostages. They needn't have been. The Palestinian soldiers could have picked other targets."

"It's very difficult to draw the line," Terzi repeats. He goes on to stress that the PLO now condemns skyjacking, though it cannot prevent the tactic from being used by splinter groups. Why does he condemn it? "It doesn't really accomplish its purpose. Realistically, attacks should be aimed at Israeli nationals or territory."

"Then why are you training IRA guerrillas?"

"We believe national liberation movements should show solidarity—but in any case we're not the ones training them. That's being done by other Arab groups."

The conversation keeps coming back to hostage taking. It's not a one-sided affair, Terzi insists. There are many Palestinians detained by the Israelis. They also are hostages. But, his visitor asks, cannot these problems be resolved through negotiation? "Diplomatic methods are fine," says Terzi, "but we will never give up the gun till we've achieved our goals."

Nevertheless it's clear that, like the larger powers, the PLO would now like to use its guns mainly as a threat. It sets great store by its observer status in the United Nations and is reluctant to jeopardize its standing in the international community. "After all," Terzi points out, "we no longer need to capture publicity. The world knows about us. We're more concerned now with solid diplomatic and military achievements."

He is firmly convinced that Israel is a racist state and seems genuinely puzzled that it should so strenuously resist attempts to secularize it. "Why do they discriminate? Why are Palestinians second-class citizens inside Israel's borders? Thousands of Palestinian men leave their wives and children every week to work outside Israel, where they can get jobs, then return on weekends. They resist Israel's attempts to force them out permanently." He sits back and strokes his beard for a moment. "Suppose Israel were to suddenly grant full citizenship rights and status to the Palestinians living within her borders. Even if she kept her occupied territories then, she would still cause—I tell you frankly—a diplomatic predicament for the PLO. In a few years these people would become assimilated into the fabric of Israeli life. It would be much harder to argue then for the necessity of a Palestinian state, or for disbanding Israel in its present form. But that just won't happen."

And if Israel were to accept a Palestinian state willing to coexist with a Jewish neighbor?

"That won't happen either," says Terzi, and the interview is over.

But already diplomatic explorations were proceeding along these lines. Terzi's own comments were carefully calculated. The former terrorists would renounce neither their earlier methods nor their principles; yet clearly there had been changes, and the violence of the frontier was less important at this moment than the symbolism of that hard, bare office on Park Avenue.

If terrorism is a technique of war, by the same token war, as Terzi suggested, has in it unmistakable elements of terrorism: the casual shooting of civilians, the bombing of cities, schools, and hospitals. Nevertheless, the rationale behind such deeds is more complex, partly because the practitioners of wartime atrocities, acting on behalf of established governments, are far less clear about their motives, in public at any rate, than terrorists are.

The evidence we have—and unfortunately we have a great deal—indicates that the strategy of wartime terrorism by belligerent governments is less well thought out, less effective, and vastly more costly in human lives than the strategies of many small, would-be revolutionary bands. During World War II a large part of this terror involved the use of the airplane. Even before the Blitz began, British and German airplane gunners had few qualms about shooting civilians and helpless airmen. In *The First Casualty*, Phillip Knightley recounts details of the air war over England: "There was nothing glamorous in the theory and nothing glamorous in the practice. The Germans fired on British pilots floating helplessly beneath their parachutes because they could, after all, be back in battle the same afternoon shooting down Germans. The RAF, equally calculating, had no compunction about destroying a Heinkel 59 seaplane with civilian markings as it was engaged in rescuing German pilots floating in the Channel, or another Heinkel 59 marked with the Red Cross. True, Air Chief Marshall Sir Hugh Dowding forbade British pilots to shoot at Germans who parachuted to safety over Britain, since it was necessary to wait only a few seconds for them to be captured, but the British pilots interpreted this order as allowing them to give the German all they had while he was still struggling out of his cockpit."

While these abuses seem to have resulted from ad hoc decisions by fighting men, the strategy of terror became official policy soon enough. It had an odd twist to begin with. Eager for America to enter the war against the Germans, Churchill searched for a German atrocity—such as the bombing of British civilians—that might inflame American public opinion and bring about a declaration of war. For a long time nothing of the kind happened and Churchill was frustrated; he could hardly order the bombing of his own people. Fortunately the Germans came to his aid through a mistake. In August of 1940, intending to bomb an oil storage depot near London, they inadvertently bombed part of London itself. The next day Churchill in reprisal ordered the bombing of Berlin, and, intentionally or not, these bombs too fell on civilian targets. Germany retaliated in kind, and the Blitz was on.

British pilots died at an alarming rate in these raids, while having only a minimal effect on the German war effort, and British antiaircraft fire killed more Englishmen at first than Germans. Convinced that more such raids, and more frequent ones, would destroy German morale, Churchill made Berlin's civilian populations—and especially its densely packed working-class areas—the primary target. Yet just as the British dug in before the German onslaught on civilian centers, so did the Germans, even though Berlin was, in Knightley's words, "the most-bombed place on earth at that time." German war production continued to increase in the face of horrors like that described by Edward R. Murrow in 1943: "Men die in the sky while others are roasted alive in their cellars. . . . This is a calculated, remorseless campaign of destruction."

Nevertheless the ferocious campaign continued on both sides throughout the war, culminating in the bombing of Dresden by the RAF on February 13, 1945. Never crucial as a center of military production, Dresden was at that time crowded with half a million refugees from Silesia, who had fled before the advancing Russian troops. Three quarters of a million incendiary bombs fell on the city that night, creating a holocaust that beggars description. It was not just that the whole city was on fire; the heat from the flames created fierce convection currents that sucked everything into their path. In Knightley's words, "At Dresden, winds approaching 100 miles an hour swept debris and people into a fire centre where the temperature exceeded 1,000 degrees centigrade. The flames ate everything organic, everything that would burn. People died by the thousands, cooked, incinerated, or suffocated. Then American planes came the next day to machine-gun survivors as they struggled to the banks of the Elbe." If, as postwar estimates suggest, over 100,000 people died in that raid, it was a destruction far in excess of the death toll at Hiroshima.

Like Hiroshima, it was emphatically not a mistake. As the Associated Press reported four days later, "Allied Air Chiefs have made the long-awaited decision to adopt deliberate terror bombings of German population centers as a ruthless expedient of hastening Hitler's doom." Many other dooms, of course, preceded Hitler's. The "long-awaited decision" had, in fact, been made much earlier in the war; it had simply become impossible for press or public to ignore by now.

The strategic usefulness of this bombing is dubious at best. Already Russian advances had crumbled Germany's eastern front, and what damage could be done to her wartime production had been done elsewhere. It is doubtful whether the bombing shortened the war by an amount sufficient to "justify" the overnight extinction of 100,000 lives. The inescapable conclusion must be that those who participated in the war, from the dogfaces to the supreme commanders, were brutalized by it, made lustful for revenge, and were no longer capable of distinguishing enemy combatants from innocent victims. Under conditions of desperation all members of the opposing side are seen as the active enemy; their only proper fate is to be destroyed. By the end of the war the press made no pretense of objectivity and little of humanity. Knightley quotes the British correspondent Ronald Monson, who became so angry after touring the concentration camp at Belsen that "I drove my car into a column of German prisoners. My God, did they scream!"

But such moral righteousness, coupled with cold-blooded brutality toward one's opponent, is precisely the attitude of the terrorist. As soon as the partisan reaches the stage where he can either deny the innocence of anyone who is not on his side or assert that such innocence is irrelevant to the over-riding issue, which is his own side's final triumph, then he is in a psychological position to commit a terrorist act, whether on behalf of a government in the context of a war or on behalf of a movement dedicated to ultimate revolution.

The contagion extends still further. If attitudes of moral superiority and belief in the necessity of violence against the innocent are shared by terrorists and governments at war, they are also appropriated by the ordinary soldier with disconcerting ease and made the basis and justification for individual forays of destruction and death. It is easy enough to see how this can happen. Through a conscious policy of dehumanizing the enemy, governments instill in citizens and soldiers alike the will to fight. Thus Germans were Huns in the First World War and Nazis in the Second. Orientals were Japs in that latter war and gooks, slopes, or slants in the most recent American venture. Common soldiers, exhorted during basic training to "Kill! Kill! Kill! Kill! Kill!" and encouraged to help their company "bag" its quota of enemy soldiers, can readily be expected to take matters into their own hands. After sufficient time, they will not only kill opposing soldiers with a gusto bordering on sadism, but will begin to define all members of the enemy nation as subhuman and therefore fair game. War correspondent Frank Harvey reported, "One F-4 fighter-bomber pilot in Danang [Vietnam] told me he thought we should start at the DMZ [demilitarized zone] and kill every man, woman and child in North Vietnam."

Such racism contributed to the ultimate destruction of the American war effort in Vietnam, for it gradually became clear to the people at home that American soldiers made virtually no distinctions between the Vietnamese they were supposed to be helping and those they were supposed to be killing. In Phillip Knightley's words, "The enemy was physically indistinguishable from the ally. Racist hate directed at Charlie Cong the enemy made no provision for exempting those Vietnamese that the United States had intervened to save. In motivating the GI to fight by appealing to his racist feelings, the United States military discovered that it had liberated an emotion over which it was to lose control. Sartre has written that American racism—anti-Negro, anti-Mexican, anti-Asian —is 'a fundamental fact which goes very deep and which existed, potentially, or in fact, long before the Vietnam war.' "

In his "Message to the Tricontinental," Ché Guevara advocated "relentless hatred of the enemy that impels us over and beyond the natural limitations of man and transforms us into effective, violent, selective, and cold killing machines. Our soldiers must be thus; a people without hatred cannot vanquish a brutal enemy. We must carry the war as far as the enemy carries it: to his home, to his centers of entertainment, in a total war." Compare this with the testimony of an American Vietnam veteran: "It wasn't like they were humans. We were conditioned to believe this was for the good of the nation, the good of our country, and anything we did was okay. And when you shot at someone you didn't think you were shooting at a human. They were a Gook or a Commie and it was okay." Another veteran recalled the killing of a twelve-year-old Vietnamese boy: "My first reaction was, I guess, you would call normal. It would be horror, pain, and when I realized that, I caught myself immediately and said 'No, you can't do that.' . . . I caught myself letting the shell down and I tightened up right away."

By 1968 such feelings were out in the open. In March of that year a United States platoon commanded by Lt. William Calley, Jr., entered the village of My Lai, rounded up the inhabitants—men, women, and children—and began spraying bullets from automatic weapons at them. Any survivors, including tiny children, were picked off individually with rifles as they stood clutching the hands of their dead parents. The job was done with grisly efficiency, and when it was over between 90 and 130 people lay dead in the moist heat, in the midst of the oddly silent jungle clearing.

It would be comforting to believe this was an isolated instance of barbarism, that Calley and his men were perverted and atypical, and that all but a few deviant American soldiers were the kind who, in the World War II stereotype, liked nothing better than to give chocolates to small village kids.

However, after sifting the published and unpublished evidence of correspondents covering Vietnam throughout the war years, Knightley concludes, "There were events equally horrifying before My Lai, and massacres on a larger scale occurred afterwards. . . . With no moral restraints against 'wasting' Vietnamese, in fact with incentives to do so, and with the understandable desire, above all, to stay alive, the American soldier in Vietnam ended up committing acts that the nation believed impossible. 'Some people think that the Japanese committed atrocities, that the Germans committed atrocities, that the Russians committed atrocities, but that the Americans don't commit atrocities,' Colonel Robert Rheault, a commander of the United States Special Forces in Vietnam, said just after My Lai. 'Well, this just isn't so. American troops are as capable as any of committing atrocities.' "

In short, war provides ample means for terrorism, means which may be employed officially, as in authorized bombing raids on civilians, or semiofficially, as when troops are encouraged to kill members of the "enemy" with little regard for their status as soldiers or noncombatants, or quite unofficially, when soldiers rape and kill civilians out of a paradoxical sense of their own power and powerlessness—a state of mind closely akin to that of the domestic hostage takers who plagued America in 1977.

Such activities, viewed over the span of a futile and demoralizing war, help to place the physical if not the political threat of terrorism in perspective. It is safe to say that since the turn of the century terrorism has neither threatened nor killed a fraction of the number of civilians who suffered in any one major war, including the war in Vietnam. To those who object that war is, after all, a special circumstance during which normally unconscionable horrors may be expected to occur and even be justified in the light of urgent national needs, the guerrilla will respond that, whether you recognize it, he too is at war, and the life-or-death considerations that impel him amply justify his depredations on innocent lives.

If he is thoughtful, he will add that his actions usually have much more strategic justification, that they are better planned in view of specific ends, than those of the bored and brutalized soldier who acts on his own. No one will deny that there are ill-advised and naïve terrorist activities, but because he operates not anonymously in a jungle under siege but openly under the scrutiny of the entire world, the terrorist very often strives to make every venture count as much as possible. The success of his movement depends on it, and if he fails he cannot easily be replaced.

His strategy may seem naïve to the point of irrationality, but it is still a strategy. One of the Japanese United Red Army terrorists justified the Lod Airport massacre performed by his comrades in this way: "Our struggle is supported by the repressed proletariat of the world. Therefore to struggle is itself good propaganda. And we believe we must perform many more such propaganda activities everywhere. At present our power is too small to be truly effective." Israel, in this view, was an agent of capitalism and American imperialism, and so an attack against anyone who offered even indirect support, such as the tourists aboard the Air France jet ready to spend their money in Israel's war economy, was an attack on the abettors of imperialism and the enemies of the people. Naïve and dangerous as it seems, this attitude should be contrasted with the official United States position, from the mid-fifties to the early seventies, that virtually any measures were acceptable in southeast Asia to prevent the overthrow of governments sympathetic to capitalism by what was seen as a monolithic Communist imperialism. By that reasoning, which sometimes found its way to dangerous heights in the American power structure, the wholesale destruction of nations potentially sympathetic to Communism might not be too high a price to pay.

Positions that at first appear highly moral have a way of coming down to issues of basic prejudice or personal or national ideology. To many Westerners, the Lod massacre seemed inherently more heinous than the My Lai massacre because the latter was committed in the context of what was billed as a war against Communism, whereas the gunners at Lod actually appeared to champion Communism. The end, in short, excuses if it does not justify the means. If we grant that case, however, then objections to terrorism as a mode of operation are moot and should be acknowledged as such. The essential difference between the Armies of the Lord and the Hounds of Hell has nothing to do with technique.

There remain individuals, and probably many of them, who will have no brief with massacres no matter who commits them. Their point of view is the more interesting one, for it leads back to one of the main concerns of this book: what can be done to reduce the levels of political violence? Whether psychological approaches, target hardening, or judicial sanctions are tried, it is clear that in a great many cases international cooperation is not only desirable but essential. It took the ambassadors of three Muslim countries to persuade Hamaas Abdul Khaalis to release the hostages he held in three separate locations in Washington, D.C. Dissident Cuban exiles stopped hijacking American airplanes to their homeland only after Havana and Washington agreed that this activity would no longer be condoned in Cuba. And when it is necessary to consider ways of arresting, trying, and convicting persons accused of political terrorism, nations inevitably turn to the debates of the United Nations.

There, however, the problem we have just examined is painfully clear: many nations are unwilling to condemn those varieties of terrorism that might benefit their interests, or to give the United Nations any power that it might use to curtail them. The United States has frequently voted against Security Council resolutions to censure Israel for acts of terrorism against her Arab neighbors, yet on many occasions has strongly condemned instances of Arab terrorism. Many Third World countries, by contrast, resist United Nations attempts to place international controls on the taking of hostages, since this is an activity that they believe, on occasion, may be useful to them.

In spite of the admittedly self-serving positions taken by many of the main participants in these debates, the major legal problems of international terrorism have received enough public discussion by now to stand out in sharp relief. Even when the emotions surrounding them are set aside it is clear that they are not easy problems. Nevertheless, they need to be dealt with before any international law on the subject of terrorism is possible. Such law is urgently needed: at present the terrorist's best refuge from prosecution is the nation that will harbor him; and arguably a major reason for the proliferation of terrorism is the lack of a suitable forum to which national minorities can bring their grievances.

VI

WHO WILL
BELL THE CAT?

JACOB SUNDBERG IS A TALL, ARISTOCRATIC SWEDE WHO
teaches law at the University of Stockholm and frequently
travels abroad to expound Sweden's legal codes and official
policies affecting terrorism. He is one of a small number of
authorities on such matters. But even he is perplexed by the
issues raised in the curious case of Vassilios Tsironis, once
a Greek politician, who in 1969 and 1970 caused a great deal
of frustration and no little embarrassment to the Swedish
government. As Sundberg tells the story it began in 1967
when, in the wake of the military junta's coup in Greece, led
by Col. George Papadopoulos, Sweden took a public stand
against the policies of the new regime, including torture and
mass political imprisonments. The ruling Social Democratic
Party in Sweden officially encouraged the Pan-Hellenic liberation movement and invited the exiled Greek leader Andreas Papandreou to direct a resistance campaign from
Swedish soil. Papandreou accepted and spent a year as a
visiting professor at the University of Stockholm before moving on to Canada. During this time the Swedish government
removed restrictions on political activity by political refugees
who had been given asylum.

At the same time, Sweden, like many other countries, adhered to the principle that residents, whether citizens or
foreigners, were bound by Swedish laws and could either be
tried for crimes committed abroad, if they also violated
Swedish law, or else extradited to the country in which those
crimes had taken place. In particular, Sweden looked with
disfavor on airplane hijacking, which was a violation of the
Swedish penal code, even though there had as yet been no
hijackings of Swedish aircraft.

Enter now Vassilios Tsironis, the founder of a Greek anti-establishment party and an avowed opponent of the Papadopoulos junta. Having been jailed several times during the first two years of the dictatorship, Tsironis decided in the summer of 1969 to leave the country for the sake of his health and the cause of future liberty in Greece. The junta denied him a passport, but Tsironis was resourceful. One summer day he took his family on a domestic flight aboard an Olympic Airways jet and, over the Bay of Corinth, hijacked the plane.

He forced it to fly to Albania, and after it landed he headed, by legal means, to Sweden, where he was given a hero's welcome. The government decided he deserved the same treatment it had accorded Papandreou; it gave him a generous allowance and quartered him and his family in Stockholm's Hotel Carlton, where officials thought he would be protected from undercover reprisals by a large city's anonymity.

Threats came, however, not from the undercover agents of the Greek colonels but, ironically, from a Swede—Sundberg himself. On November 5, 1969, he wrote to the chief state prosecutor pointing out that Tsironis had violated Sweden's antihijacking law in the process of leaving Greece, and inquiring why he wasn't being prosecuted since, in his exile, the only courts of competent jurisdiction were Swedish courts. That stumped the prosecutor. He thought about it for a week and then began an investigation. Tsironis shortly found himself indicted for hijacking, hotel fraud, and assaulting a policeman (this last charge incurred as he was being arrested on the other charges).

The trial of Vassilios Tsironis in Sweden resembled that of Bobby Seale in the United States. Tsironis fired his lawyer, then fired the lawyer's replacement. He accused the court and the prosecutor of torture and corruption. He threatened to scream throughout the trial and eventually was taken out of the courtroom and placed in an adjoining room in Långholmen Prison. In passing sentence the baffled court observed: "Tsironis has refused to cooperate in the proceedings.

. . . He has behaved in an extremely disturbing way before the Court and he has in no way obeyed the directives that have been given to maintain order and carry out the trial. . . . He has refused to talk with his defense counsel and he has not even made contact with the interpreter that was appointed for the case." Sundberg comments: "The general public in Sweden never realized the contradiction that had so infuriated Dr. Tsironis. It required several years and a hijacking taking place in Sweden herself and involving an SAS aircraft for the Swedish government to seriously undertake to harmonize its support of foreign rebel movements in the world with the worldwide fight against hijackings."

Simply stated, the contradiction comes down to this: how should a country, committed to granting asylum to those persecuted for political crimes in their native countries, and even to encouraging their activities against repressive governments, treat those refugees whose "political crimes" were also terrorist acts?

The notion of political crime is an ancient one and was the basis for some of the first extradition treaties among nations. To judge by the evidence we have, early states were not so interested in recovering common criminals who had fled their borders—in fact, the less seen of such troublemakers, the better—but they felt their stability threatened by crimes of disloyalty and therefore were anxious to make an example of political offenders. Those who fled might league themselves with foreign powers against their native land. To prevent that, they should be returned whenever possible. Thus in one of the oldest surviving documents in diplomatic history, Ramses II of Egypt and the Hittite ruler Hattusilis III, having just fought a war, covenanted in 1269 B.C. to return the disloyal subjects of either party who had fled to the other. In the Middle Ages England and Scotland entered into such a treaty in 1174, and France and Savoy did likewise in 1303. This practice found its way into the classic formulations of international law by Hugo Grotius in the seventeenth century.

That a political offender in one country might be a virtuous defender of human rights in another did not seriously occur to Europeans until the last decade of the eighteenth century. The ideas of the Enlightenment plus two revolutions, the French and the American, persuaded political thinkers that some sovereigns had no moral imperative to rule and, lacking the consent of the governed, could justly be overthrown. But if such a principle was recognized by progressive nations, where was the justice in arresting the individual who had worked, albeit unsuccessfully, toward that revolution, and forcibly returning him to the one country in the world most likely to reward him with a painful death? Translating this reasoning into practice, Belgium in 1833 pioneered in passing a law providing that political offenders were not subject to extradition. Other countries followed suit. By the last quarter of the nineteenth century the wheel had come full circle: political crime, once the major basis for extradition, was now the major exception to extradition treaties among most European nations. Moreover, it was left to the courts of the state providing asylum to determine whether the offense of the fugitive was political. It would not be possible, therefore, for a nation to get back a "prodigal son" on the pretext that his offense was only a common crime like murder and then try and convict him for a political transgression. In the atmosphere of national rivalry prevailing in Europe in the late nineteenth century the disaffected were thus able to foment revolution, fail, and then flee to a safe haven in a neighboring state. Human rights, at least in theory, prevailed over another nation's security.

What was a political offense remained in doubt, however, since definitions were rarely provided in law and courts offered varying interpretations. As time went on, nations became uncomfortably aware that international stability as well as internal order were threatened if an anarchist might shoot a prime minister, then flee to impunity in the bosom of another country. Belgium, in fact, learned the lesson early in the wake of its "political offender" legislation of 1833. Twenty years later there was a plot on the life of Napoleon III. A group of French nationals tried to blow up a train on which he was riding. Their attempt failed and, with the police hot on their heels, they requested asylum. Naturally enough, France demanded extradition. Most of Europe sympathized with France. The Belgian parliament responded by enacting in 1855 a curious exception to its extradition treaty called the "attentat clause," which has since been adopted by a large number of Western countries: "No act shall be considered a political crime or connected with such a crime if it is an attack upon the person of the head of a foreign government or of the members of his family, when this attack takes the form of either murder, assassination or poisoning." In short, in many countries it became possible to flee the consequences of a great variety of antigovernment acts, but assassination was not a political crime and thus remained an extraditable offense.

In this way Europe's most exclusive club, the club of kings, took care of its own. The attitude was openly acknowledged by England's King Edward VII in 1905 as he recalled the 1903 assassination of King Alexander of Serbia: "My particular business is that of being king. King Alexander was also by his trade a king. As you see, we belonged to the same guild, as labourers or professional men. I cannot be indifferent to the assassination of a member of my guild. We should be obliged to shut up our businesses if we, the kings, were to consider the assassination of kings as of no consequence at all."

Where does that leave the terrorist of today? His position is still curiously anomalous, for a number of the activities that commonly get him into trouble are not formally recognized as political crimes by most governments. When a German named Richard Eckermann fled to Guatemala in 1928 after ordering the death of one Fritz Beyer, who tried to join the secret army organization to which Eckermann belonged and was suspected of being a spy, Germany requested his extradition. Eckermann demurred, protesting that his was a political crime. Not so, decided the Guatemalan court: "Universal law qualifies as political crimes sedition, rebellion, and other offenses which tend to change the form of government or the persons who compose it; but it cannot be admitted that ordering a man killed with treachery, unexpectedly and in an uninhabited place, without form of trial or authority to do it, constitutes a political crime." The activities of modern terrorists might have posed even more difficulties for the court. If a terrorist kidnaps an ambassador or a cabinet minister, is that an act of treason? If not, is it a political crime at all? And if it is not a political crime for purposes of claiming asylum, has it any more weight when it comes to trial than the kidnapping of a private citizen?

In international law, a crime is what nations recognize to be a crime. Most have agreed to consider murder in another country as serious as murder on their own territory; thus not only is murder recognized as a crime, there is reciprocity in the way nations choose to regard it. For this reason it is called a common crime. Political crime, however, is different in that while the general category, such as treason, is recognized by all nations, specific manifestations have quite different values from one country to another. A treasonous act against Israel may horrify and outrage the Israelis while the Russians feel indifferent and the Syrians may be jubilant. A purely political crime, in fact, which entails no taint of a common crime of violence or fraud, results from nothing more than the exercise of the faculty of speech—to divulge a secret, incite a crowd, talk to an enemy. Because these acts are not acts against common humanity but only against the state whose interests will suffer in their wake, other states are reluctant to condemn the perpetrator and may in fact praise him. Following these lines, the international legal scholar M. Cherif Bassiouni offers not a definition but a test: "A purely political offense is one whereby the conduct of the actor manifests an exercise in freedom of thought, expression and belief (by words, symbolic acts or writings not inciting to violence), [or] freedom of association and religious practice which are in violation of law designed to prohibit such conduct."

It would seem it is the easiest thing in the world to be charged with a political offense, as Daniel Ellsberg learned, but to be a terrorist is something else again. For a terrorist may engage in none of the classic political offenses and yet wreak very disturbing damage, both personal and political, in the country he chooses to attack. Admittedly his offense would still be an offense if it were not politically motivated, as the trials of the many nonpolitical imitators of terrorists in the United States attest, but the avowedly political motive lends color to the act, making it more heinous in the eyes of the offended nation, and often mitigating it in the eyes of nations sympathetic to the terrorist. Common crimes with political overtones can thus be called "complex crimes": to the extent that they are common, nations will agree that they should be prosecuted; to the extent that they are political, nations will disagree and often try to avoid the issue. So much was this the case in Sweden that the country forgot it was giving a hero's welcome to a hijacker until reminded that hijacking was against Swedish as well as Greek law. And when in the early fifties some crew members aboard a Yugoslav airplane overpowered other crew members and hijacked the plane to Switzerland to escape from their native land, the Swiss court declared that the political motive could "excuse, if not justify, the injury to private property." Yet in the 1941 trial of Youssef Said Abu Dourrah for a "political" murder allegedly committed in England, the Palestine court observed, "We know of nothing in the criminal law of this country or of England that creates a specific offense called political murder."

At this point the legal argument becomes very subtle. Murder, to be sure, has always been a crime admitting various degrees of severity depending on the intentions of the murderer. Was the murder premeditated? Was it impulsive? Was it committed in a condition of temporary insanity? Was it done in reaction to a perceived threat to life and limb? Surely, a political motive might also be extenuating (or complicating, depending on your point of view). Not so, says the jurist. "The element of intent required for all serious crimes bears upon the state of mind of the actor at the time the *actus reus* [the act] was committed. As such the *mens rea*

[mind] does not contemplate the reason why, the ultimate purpose, or the motivating factors which brought about this state of mind. Certainly motive is relevant in proving intent, but it is not an element of the crime and, therefore, has no bearing on whether or not the actor's overall conduct, the accompanying mental state and its resulting harm, will be characterized a crime. It will, however, be relevant in the determination of the sentence."

By this reasoning, when a man is charged with murder, the fact that his victim was an ambassador and his intent the disruption of the ambassador's state should have no bearing on his eligibility for asylum or, once he is brought to trial, on the prosecution of the case. On the other hand, it may result in his receiving a light sentence if he is tried in a country sympathetic to his purpose, or in his being hanged if he is tried by the ambassador's government. Recognizing this likelihood, prosecutors in the state in which such a murderer seeks refuge can hardly be indifferent to his pleas for asylum on the ground that his is a political crime, even though the political motive was just ruled out as a basis for deciding on extradition! Evidently the law is of two minds.*

Such was the dilemma faced briefly by France in the case of Abu Daoud. Daoud had not sought refuge in France; he had not needed it. Long an official in the Palestine Liberation Organization, and suspected of plotting the terrorist action at the 1972 Munich Olympics that resulted in the deaths of eleven Israeli athletes, he arrived in Paris in January 1977 with a Palestinian delegation to attend the funeral of Mohmoud Saleh, a bookseller and Palestinian activist. He assumed he was on safe territory, since France has long maintained friendly relations with the Arab world. Apparently the French government assumed the same thing, but the French counterintelligence network hadn't gotten the word. The agents were efficient and polite: a knock at the door, a few quiet words, identification presented, and then Daoud found himself being

---

* Of course, there is more than one law. Not a few countries have policies resembling the provision in West Germany's constitution which expressly grants asylum to the politically persecuted.

trundled down to headquarters in an inconspicuous car.

He was angry; the whole matter was distasteful and offensive to him. Since when was France waging a holy war against Palestinian interests, and Abu Daoud in particular? What had he done to France? Those were not the only questions he might have asked, but Daoud was not questioning his conscience. Such questions as he did ask were to no avail. After a brief hearing Abu Daoud was forcibly detained.

Suddenly several nations and groups were expressing contradictory points of view with as much heat as diplomacy allows. The French police who were responsible for the arrest apparently bore a grudge against the PLO stemming from underground warfare in which terrorists had killed some police officials. Whatever the diplomatic stance of their government, they were crowing among themselves. Israel wanted Daoud extradited to Israel to stand trial for the murder of Israeli nationals. West Germany said it wanted him sent there to be tried for murders committed on German soil. Privately Bonn was less than eager to stir up the controversy such a proceeding would inevitably provoke. Doubtless there would be terrorist reprisals if Daoud were even tried in Germany, let alone convicted, and in particular the Baader-Meinhof group could be expected to spring into action, causing a new wave of internal unrest. With no such domestic anxieties but a general commitment to support Israel's interests, the United States backed the requests for extradition and trial.

Meanwhile the Arab countries maintained a discreet silence. It would have been awkward to argue for Daoud's release if he was in fact to be charged with the common crime of murder. On the other hand, it wasn't necessary for them to protest too much. French president Valéry Giscard d'Estaing was about to visit Saudi Arabia. Daoud's pending trial could have made his visit distinctly uncomfortable. France imports nearly four fifths of its oil from the Middle East and supplies Egypt and other Arab nations with Mirage jets, Alouette helicopters, rockets, AMX-30 tanks, and other weapons. In the midst of such a delicate and profitable arsenal the Daoud trial could have exploded like a grenade. Should

France hold on to him or toss him to Germany or Israel?

Within four days the decision came down to the courts: release him. They did. Daoud flew to Algeria, where he promptly held a news conference denouncing Israel.

In the ensuing international uproar Israel protested loudest; Germany also complained, though observers suspected there was private relief among officials there. The United States made moral pronouncements and lodged protests with the French government. The official French story was that the German extradition papers were technically deficient, but few people bought that explanation, since under French law Daoud could have been held more than two weeks while the papers were corrected. The news media made sure no one missed the point. After listening to expressions of righteous outrage from the United States, Giscard d'Estaing retorted that France didn't presume to preach lessons in international law or morality to other countries and shouldn't have to listen to any. He made no apologies and offered no explanation. The newspaper *Le Monde* summed up: "When you have a police service that does not take orders and a judiciary that does, and a Government that opts for political expediency in the face of domestic and world opinion, it adds up to an unfortunate mess." And *The New York Times* found it "almost inexplicable" that Daoud, accused of "one of the most notorious terrorist acts of recent years," should be set free.

In fact there has been a tendency in French legal thought, cogently expounded by Jacques Léauté of the Institute for Criminology at the Sorbonne, to treat terrorists not as criminals but as political prisoners whose "guilt" is of a different order. Under this theory it is not relevant that they have violated the laws laid down for citizens in peacetime; what matters is that they are belligerents in a self-declared war. Thus as offenders they are of interest only to the opposing state. It is as if an American army deserter, who as a killer of Vietnamese would have been taken prisoner by North Vietnam, might find refuge in Canada and have no fear of being tried for his activities as a combatant. (Of course, the problem is complicated in the case of terrorism in that any nation may be a battleground.) The full implications of this "prisoner of war" theory are not universally accepted in France, and they certainly have not taken hold in international law, though they have been suggested in cases where the terrorist action was confined to the territory of the attacked state. That was not the case, of course, in Munich, yet the rationale could have been extended with some ingenuity: after all, the French government was embarrassed by a politically explosive arrest. For if Daoud could be thought of as a prisoner of war, it was clearly not France's war. The struggle was between the Palestinians, or more broadly, the entire Arab world, and Israel, and although the French government was aware of the ugliness of Daoud's purported offense against Israel, it was also aware of some ugly attacks by Israeli agents on Arabs, such as the case of the exploding telephone, mentioned earlier. By this reasoning it was a mistake to capture Daoud at all. He should be returned to his own camp if he wished to go. He did, and he was.

France's decision was a cheap way out, dictated far more by politics than by theory. No government official even tried to justify it. It could have been rationalized only by conceding that a terrorist is entitled by virtue of his political motives to the status of a combatant and that, no matter to what territory he extends the conflict, if he kills civilian nationals of another country his offense is only against that country (with which he says he is at war) and not against humanity in general. That position, however, would place terrorism outside existing international law, which seeks to punish all offenses against the public order. Immediate trial, extradition, or freedom: what are the merits of the conflicting claims?

Consider the general case: a national of one country (in this case one without undisputed territory of its own) is alleged to have a role in the deaths of citizens of a second country. These people were killed, however, within the territory of a third country, and the accused terrorist is now (before his release) in the hands of yet a fourth country. Granted that he should be tried, who should try him? Even if the Palestinians, at this point an inchoate nation, had the competence or the desire to try Daoud for the murder of the Israeli athletes, their claim to him would be the thinnest in international law. It would be based on the *principle of personality*—that is, that jurisdiction (the right to conduct a trial) is tied to the nationality of the person who commits the crime. According to this theory a nation has the right to try its own citizens for whatever offenses they may commit against anyone else, anywhere else in the world. Even leaving aside the question whether such a trial could possibly be unbiased in this case, this claim is rarely pressed or honored; as a practical matter there are much stronger claims to jurisdiction.

Israel would have a more convincing case. It would be based on the *protective principle*: the notion that a state has the right to protect its citizens, wherever they may be, by taking actions against anyone who seeks to harm them. Such a principle is often invoked, even without going through the legal machinery of extradition, to secure a sought-after offender who has taken refuge in another country or to rescue one's own nationals threatened abroad. It was on this principle that Israeli commandos flew into Uganda under cover of night in July 1976, shot nineteen Ugandan guards and the five terrorists who were holding Israeli and other citizens hostage, and made off with them before Ugandan president Idi Amin even knew the raid had taken place. It was on this principle that the United States sent ships and planes into Cambodian waters in May 1975 to rescue an empty ship— the S.S. Mayaguez—and its crew who, it turned out, were aboard a Thai fishing boat in Cambodian hands, and not in need of rescue beause they were being voluntarily returned to the Americans. It was on this principle also that Israeli agents hunted down Adolf Eichmann in Argentina in 1961 and dragged him back to Israel, where he was called to justice in a spectacular trial, condemned, and hanged for the murder of millions of Jews in German concentration camps during World War II. In this case, Israel's claim to Daoud would be damaged only by the sense in the international community that passions against him might run so high in Israel that he would not receive a fair trial there.

Probably the strongest claim could be put forward by West Germany. It would be based on the *territorial principle*—the notion that every country is responsible for the welfare of all persons within its borders, whether they are its citizens or not, and that in order to protect that welfare a nation may prosecute anyone who commits a crime on its territory. Considering further that Daoud could have received a less inflamed trial in Germany than in Israel, the German request for extradition would have been the most plausible one from nearly all points of view.

A very weak claim might have been put forward by France, had she been so inclined, and then only if other nations had declined to request extradition. France might have argued that Daoud was charged with an offense against humanity and that, in such cases, a nation has the obligation either to extradite or to punish (*aut dedere aut punire*). In this case, of course, there was no lack of parties with the desire, at least officially, and the legal justification to conduct a trial, nor was it unlikely that Daoud would have received a fair trial in Germany.

In the absence of an international court with automatic jurisdiction in cases of political terrorism involving more than one country, such legal principles provide the only means of making sure terrorists are prosecuted. The general principle recited above, under which all nations who have suspected terrorists in custody are obliged to try them or else to extradite them to a country that will try them, is the only common ground in international law (which is based on mutual agreements between countries) that assures that terrorists will be brought to justice.

By allowing some latitude in the choice of a trial site, and thus increasing the chances that the trial will be fair, this principle actually implements a second principle, one which could be better realized by a genuine international court, if such a body should ever come into being. That principle is the separation of ends from means. Stated more fully, it says that a well-governed society provides avenues for achieving social and political goals and that these avenues, which are lawful, must be adhered to by citizens, even if they are more frustrating, time consuming, inefficient, or apparently futile than other means which are unlawful. It implies further that unlawful means cannot be made more tolerable simply by invoking the honorable ends they were intended to bring about, nor can they be made to seem more abhorrent if the associated ends are repugnant to the majority. In practical terms the trial of an airline hijacker should, by this principle, focus strictly on the deed itself. What is relevant is that the terrorist is accused of a threat to the public order and safety. His intention to use the hijacking as a way to provoke internal unrest or dissatisfaction with the current government—or even to promote revolution—should be irrelevant to the trial. If fomenting revolution is a crime, then that is a matter for a separate charge, but it is not grounds for viewing the hijacking itself as a graver crime than the provisions of the law allow. One ought not to treat the terrorist more severely because one opposes his aim or let him off lightly because one supports him. Such a separation of ends from means, legal theorists argue, is fundamental to the principles of liberal democracy championed in Western nations.

It is obvious, of course, that such principles are breached by many of the countries that subscribe to them at least as often as they are by terrorists. International illegalities up to and including war are sanctioned at times when the "national interest" is thought to require drastic measures; on the other hand, individuals whose "offense" is only to make the powerful uncomfortable are harassed and persecuted in more or less subtle ways. America's Black Power advocates spent some very uncomfortable years in the 1960's being hassled by local police and the FBI, while American planes systematically dropped napalm on Vietnamese civilians in the name of national security. Nevertheless, the principle stands, and it is particularly useful in dealing with terrorism, where the techniques of common crime are deployed for political purposes that often carry more emotional weight than the immediate consequences of the crimes themselves. Up to now no bilateral or multilateral extradition conventions between nations have dealt with the problem of terrorism. Perhaps that is just as well, since the very term means radically different things in different countries. However, numerous attempts have been made in international law to deal with the issues raised by cases like the Daoud case or the case of Dr. Tsironis. These were perhaps best summed up and elaborated in a document produced in 1972 by the Third International Symposium sponsored by the International Institute for Advanced Criminal Sciences. It set forth the following principles:

1 / An alleged terrorist offender in custody should be effectively prosecuted and punished or else extradited to a state which requested him and intends to prosecute him.

2 / Extradition to a requesting state should be granted if the state with custody chooses not to prosecute, unless an international criminal court is created with jurisdiction over such matters, in which case the accused should be surrendered to the court's jurisdiction.

3 / All states should be vested with universal jurisdiction with respect to crimes of terrorism.

4 / Whenever a state other than the state in which the act of terrorism was committed seeks to prosecute a terrorist, a reasonable number of observers from interested states and international organizations should be allowed to see the evidence and attend all proceedings.

5 / Whenever extradition is contemplated, the ideological motives of the accused should not be the sole basis for the granting of asylum or for denying the extradition request.

6 / If the act at issue involves grave crimes, extradition should be granted regardless of the ideological motives of the actor.

7 / In all other cases, when a grave common crime has not been committed and the defendant alleges he is being charged with a political crime and thus should be immune

to extradition, the court making the decision must weigh the harm committed against the values the defendant was seeking to preserve and the means he employed in relation to the goal he sought.*

8 / In the event of multiple extradition requests for the same offender, priority should be given to the state relying on territorial jurisdiction in its request (that is, that state in whose boundaries the crime was committed), followed by the state relying on the theory of prosecuting fundamental national interests.

9 / The rights of the individual in extradition proceedings must always be upheld and he or she should not be precluded from raising any defenses available under extradition law and other relevant aspects of national and international law.

10 / Extradition should not be granted when the individual sought is to be tried by an exceptional tribunal or under a procedure in patent violation of fundamental human rights. In such cases, however, the state with custody must prosecute the accused.

11 / To prevent circumstances from arising in which states seeking an alleged terrorist will resort to extralegal measures to secure him, extradition procedures should be expedited but without sacrificing the protections afforded to the individuals, and states that do not choose to extradite should prosecute their prisoners without delay.

12 / Finally, judges, public officials, lawyers, and others who may become involved with terrorists in the course of their duties should become familiar with international criminal law, in particular those provisions relating to the extradition of those charged with terrorism.

In spite of the wide discretion granted on key issues (for example, to courts that must weigh the political goals of the offender against the harm he has caused), such draft conventions are an important step toward generally accepted

---

* Note that here, at least in extradition hearings, jurists are willing, despite cherished principles, to let the end justify the means.

provisions in international law governing the treatment of suspected terrorists. However, they founder on a fundamental issue: not every nation wants to prosecute terrorists because not every nation believes the actions associated with them are reprehensible. In particular, Third World nations object to the attempts of United Nations committees to codify the sentiments of the powerful nations and enforce them upon the rest of the world. Revolutionary struggle is too much a part of the Third World. Terrorism is a technique that may be needed.

In the late fall of 1976 the Sixth Committee of the United Nations General Assembly debated a West German resolution on hostage taking. It appeared innocuous enough. In the cautious manner of United Nations proposals it offered only to establish a framework for developing an international convention. Its purpose was to cast about for language that the assembled delegates would find acceptable and which could ultimately be codified and brought before the General Assembly for a vote. Specifically, it suggested defining hostage taking as an offense in international law, and requiring states that have seized a known hostage taker either to prosecute him or to extradite him.

At this point a number of Third World countries raised objections. They did not like the presupposition that hostage taking was an offense against civilized society and therefore a form of behavior to be punished. That might sometimes be the case, said the delegate of the United Arab Emirates, but in other circumstances it might not. As the debate proceeded, the reasoning behind this sentiment gradually clarified. The government of Libya offered an amendment stating that it was the taking of *innocent* hostages that was condemned. Somalia observed that under some circumstances it might be good to kidnap the members of "criminal" governments. It added that an absolute requirement of prosecution or extradition would be a violation of territorial sovereignty. The Algerian delegate concurred. Sometimes such acts are reprehensible, he agreed, but sometimes not. Each case must be judged individually. No single rule laid down in international law could be expected to solve the problem.

To this the delegate from the Central African Republic raised the objection that was in many people's minds: what's the point of specifying *innocent* hostages? Was not a hostage by definition innocent? Would it not, in fact, be a good idea to require that the country in which a hostage-taking episode occurred bend all possible efforts to the freeing of those hostages? But the Tanzanian delegate had a ready response: hostages, indeed, need not be innocent. Suppose a person like John Vorster of South Africa or Ian Smith of Rhodesia were taken hostage and brought to Tanzania. Could such a person be called innocent? Could the government of Tanzania work toward his release, or even cooperate in it? The questions were rhetorical, of course. Tanzania would not support such a resolution.

As delegates from Iraq, Yugoslavia, Mali, and Zambia spoke in support of the Libyan amendment, it became clear that there was confusion between a hostage-taking venture and the taking of a prisoner of war. The distinction, of course, is that a hostage is held in exchange for a specific concession by the enemy government. A prisoner, in theory, is not a medium of exchange—at least not until the conclusion of the war, when his release may depend on an exchange agreement between the warring parties. In international politics this distinction is only partly helpful, for various Third World nations still wish to reserve the right to capture prominent individuals perceived as dangerous and then use them to disrupt the enemy nation by either keeping them from their constituency or threatening dire consequences if certain demands, such as the release of other political prisoners, are not met.

As a result of such attitudes by smaller nations, which reflect an acute perception of themselves as weak partners in world alliances in need of all the leverage they can swing, including that provided by the holding of hostages, no significant action was taken on this occasion by the United Nations to further the passage of an international law concerning terrorism. This stalemate was actually a victory for several Third World countries, whose leaders could easily imagine a time when it might be necessary for them to resort to terror tactics to achieve desired social and political goals, in the face of the massive power insensitively wielded by the nuclear nations.

When all is said and done, can United Nations resolutions or multilateral treaties stem the tide of terrorism? There is no easy answer to that question, but it is difficult to be optimistic. There is some evidence that extradition treaties can succeed in reducing certain terrorist crimes in some parts of the globe. After the conclusion in 1969 of an extradition agreement between the United States and Cuba covering skyjacking crimes, and the return of six skyjackers to the United States to face charges, the incidence of air piracy by Cuban exiles bent on returning to their homeland declined dramatically. But the worldwide rate of airplane hijackings continued to rise until the beginning of 1973, when electronic inspection stations were set up at all the major airports in the world. After that point skyjackings fell off for a while, but other terrorist crimes, notably the kidnapping of prominent persons, continued to rise and spread to include more and more corporation officials as well as government representatives. In 1976, business sources maintained, twenty-seven major terrorist incidents involved U.S. businessmen or company facilities. Although such figures are not easy to prove or disprove, it is alleged that nearly 40 percent of targeted victims around the world were Americans. Since 1970, the number of persons killed by terrorist attacks has increased nearly fivefold, and the number wounded has increased over fourfold. It hardly seems, then, that the deterrent effects of international law are operating very effectively. As fast as one chops heads off the hydra, new ones grow to replace them.

Quite aside from the effect of punishment, the fear of merely getting caught and prosecuted operates as an effective deterrent for a large number of crimes. But because terrorism, unlike any of the "pure" offenses that it resembles, is essentially a "sacrificial" crime in which the offender has quite other interests at stake besides his own welfare, the terrorist's calculations are different from the criminal's, and the laws designed to reduce the incidence of such crime have a different effect. The terrorist is concerned not with whether he can get off scot-free, but with whether his ultimate object (the freeing of prisoners, or publicity for his cause) can be achieved even if he does get caught, prosecuted, and sentenced.

For that reason the primary effect of international conventions covering prosecution and extradition for terrorism is to assert once again the rule of law in the face of systematic, politically motivated lawlessness. Such conventions thus make a statement of principle, however helpless they are in deterring the dedicated terrorist. But they can have an added benefit: since, as we have seen, every well-publicized genuine terrorist act brings in its wake a number of imitators without clear political ambitions and often with purely pecuniary motives, well-worded and rigorously enforced laws at least weed out the large numbers of "imitation terrorists" who, unlike authentic ones, are usually deterred and discouraged by the convincing likelihood that they will be caught and prosecuted. Persons concerned with problems of criminal justice in general would therefore welcome the passage of a multilateral antiterrorist resolution in the United Nations. Persons concerned with the abatement of terrorism usually recognize that the main benefit of such debates and resolutions is to move the United Nations very slowly closer to the establishment of a world court empowered to hear cases involving the interaction of two or more countries or their citizens. In theory at least, such a court, its jurisdiction recognized in advance by treaty, would operate far more efficiently and fairly than even the most well-oiled extradition machinery.

But the dilemma faced by the authorities who have caught a terrorist is still not resolved. If he is to be tried in a court of law, what should be the charges, and what the punishment? Most jurists agree that terrorism is a complex crime: an action against life or property but with political motives, in which the taking of the life or the destruction of the property is actually incidental to the disruption of a state. If the terrorist is to be tried for the bare act and not the accompanying motive, on what theory of punishment is he sentenced? (We will look at this matter more closely in the next chapter, but for the moment let us consider punishment as only one of a range of possible responses.) If, on the other hand, the terrorist is tried on the basis of his political motives, his sentence may be more or less severe depending on how tolerant the court is of political dissent and incipient or full-blown revolt. A nation that feels insecure is likely to deal severely with political crimes, as America dealt with the Rosenbergs in the 1950's or as Russia deals with outspoken dissidents via house arrest, exile, or psychiatric wards. A country that is sufficiently self-confident, however, may adopt the attitude espoused by M. Léauté: that a terrorist is to be regarded simply as a member of an opposing army; he is your sworn enemy for the duration of hostilities, but at bottom he is not a bad man and, but for this distressing ideological difference, he might actually be a very decent person. Admittedly, then, he must be incapacitated, otherwise he may do your country irreparable damage; but while he is in custody he should be treated with respect and provided with all decent amenities short of freedom.

Both of these positions, which urge confinement of the convicted terrorist, though for different reasons and probably with different kinds of treatment, might be characterized as middle-ground positions, the first looking toward the right, the second toward the left. On either side of these there are more extreme positions. One, which is now and then urged in print, argues that the only good terrorist is a dead terrorist: the way to cure the disease is to kill the germs. The appeal of this approach lies in its finality and in the seeming justice of retribution. As the terrorist killed others, so he himself ought to be killed and in this way the threat he posed to society is removed at a stroke. But aside from the humanitarian argument that a life cannot answer for a life, there are two more pragmatic objections (though not necessarily better because of that). The first is that terrorist groups have genuine power, however small it is, and to put a captured terrorist to death is to invite retaliation in kind against the innocent. The second is that it is a mistake to regard terrorism as a gratuitous outpouring of hostility by a few disturbed people. Rather, it is usually a desperate response to a problem that has resisted solution by any other means. In an interview with Gerald McKnight, Bobby Seale, head of the Black Panthers, was eloquent on the subject: "Violence is perpetrated against us, the oppressed people, by the fascist system. But violence in terms of guns and billy clubs is only one form. Violence is also done to twenty million predominantly black people in this country by bringing many of them, including children, to starvation. By ignoring the dilapidation of their housing—I mean rats, biting children! That's caused by politicians and representatives who promised to solve the problem and didn't do it. That is violence, too. Violence comes in many forms.

"So. It is not isolated to 'defend yourself with a gun.' You defend yourself with a gun when you are unjustly and wrongfully attacked. . . . The final blow was a fourteen-year-old girl going to school with some books when a policeman was around the campus. She weighed 110 pounds and the policeman 210 pounds. He had a billy club, a radio, handcuffs, bullets and a gun on him. And he took a billy club and crushed that girl's head with it. He put her in the hospital for two months with a brain concussion because he said she'd kicked at him. A 110 pound girl and a 210 pound officer of the law! No, he was an officer of racism and fascism."

Such anger, growing out of such causes, cannot be extinguished by snuffing out the leaders of a physical revolt against a government and its policies. But it is a rare society or government that moves spontaneously toward social justice when faced with an unkind reminder. Movement comes slowly, for powerful interests oppose it. Conditions of social unbalance, therefore, tend to create suffering on the part of both the haves and the have-nots before they are changed.

The other extreme solution is to recognize what a very few people say is obvious: that nothing you can do to a terrorist has a significant effect on the incidence of terrorism in the world, and nothing short of killing a terrorist will keep him from being a terrorist again if he is so inclined. The obvious response to this perception, says Louk Hulsman of the University of Rotterdam, is to decriminalize terrorism, to cease prosecuting terrorists, and to exert our efforts, instead, to correct the social evils that have given rise to terrorist groups and terrorist acts in the first place. It is very difficult to argue with such a position, apart from stating the obvious fact that it is politically impossible. It *may* be true that such a policy would give rise to increased terrorist behavior, but we have no evidence that this is so. It may be that marginal groups now held in check by the threat of punishment would cut loose if that threat were removed, but it is equally arguable that the threat of punishment has done nothing to keep marginal groups in check so far. In order to discriminate rationally among these alternatives—which are alternative ways of regarding terrorists as well as alternative ways of treating them—we need to look more closely both at the nature of the punishments and at the attitudes of the terrorists being punished.

VII

THE TERRORIST
IN CAPTIVITY

VERY EARLY IN THE MORNING OF SATURDAY, SEPTEMBER 27, 1975, three young prisoners were led out of Carabanahel Prison in Madrid and driven under guard to a military barracks north of the city. There, outside in the cool air, a squad of police trained rifles on Ramon García and José Luis Sanchez Bravo. On a signal, they pulled the triggers. Next, José Francesco Baena Alonso was stood in the execution place. A civil guard squad aimed their rifles and fired. Then a detail stepped forward, picked up the bodies, and carted them off for burial.

At the same time, near the main prison in Burgos, Spain, police shot Angel Otaegui Echeverría; and in an isolated wooded area north of Barcelona, Juan Paredes Manotas, twenty-one years old, faced a firing squad of civil guardsmen and began singing the Basque nationalist hymn "Basque Soldier." Before he finished the hymn he was cut down by bullets.

In this way the waning Franco regime maintained its unpopular dominance over the Basque people. The five young men executed were part of a group of eleven originally condemned to death for killing police or members of the civil guard. Each of the eleven belonged to one of the two Basque revolutionary organizations: the ETA (*Euzkadi ta Askatasuna*, or Basque National Independence Party) or the Revolutionary Antifascist Patriotic Front. Their grievances against Spain for their treatment as an ethnic community were of long standing and had aroused sympathy throughout much of the Western world. Now they wanted independence. Earlier, on March 2, 1974, Franco had ordered the use of the garotte to execute two men, a young Catalan anarchist convicted of killing a policeman and a convicted killer of a civil guards-man. Inherited from medieval times, the garotte is an iron collar which the executioner tightens around the victim's neck until he dies of strangulation or a broken neck. Now, in re-sponse to protests and demonstrations in major cities through-out Europe, Franco commuted the death sentences of six of the eleven condemned persons and ordered that the remaining five should receive the more "dignified and honorable" death before the firing squad. To avoid charges that the executions were killings prompted by passion and a lust for revenge, he ordered further that those accused of killing civil guardsmen should be shot by the police, and vice versa. It didn't fool anyone. People rioted in the streets from Madrid to Geneva. First through social protest and later through terrorist actions, the Basques had successfully called attention to Franco's failure to address their grievances, and now the reaction to these executions announced to the world the impotence of repression before a strongly motivated civil rebellion.

The problem of Franco's Spain was apparent to all because his regime was out of sympathy with other people's social ideas, but it is only a striking example of a general problem confronting every country that sets about to try, convict, and punish an accused terrorist. The rule of law, it is felt, requires that acts against the state be punished; yet acts which are fueled by a social rather than personal grievance imply a defect in the functioning of the state and the need for accommoda-tion, not retaliation. A state that persists in exacting punish-ment for an attempt, however violent, to right a social ill runs the risk of seeming bent on revenge rather than reform and thereby feeding the discontent, however much the trial accords with due process, however "fair" the punishment.

Experience with plea bargaining, psychiatric treatment im-posed instead of imprisonment, and executive pardons has taught most Americans and Europeans that the strict rule of law can be bent to fit popular perceptions of the seriousness of the offense involved and the gravity of the threat posed by the offender. If such exceptions are not often made in the case of accused terrorists, it is because social sentiment still finds the offenses weighty and punishment in some form necessary. At least four kinds of social attitudes and expectations surround the idea of imprisonment; often they are held simultaneously.

Most primitive, but still powerful, is the notion of retribution—the conviction that society has both the right and the duty to cause the offender pain in proportion to the pain caused by his initial offense. Through the impersonal operation of laws the offender feels the full weight of social control. It is the idea of retribution rather than any modern theory of correctional effectiveness that lies behind the penalty provisions of most criminal laws, whose severity varies with the presumed seriousness of the offense. Particularly in cases where strong emotions are aroused, as in murders and sex offenses, the doctrine of retribution still appears to have overwhelming public support.

Next is the concept of deterrence: the notion that a potential offender, seeing the fate of an actual offender who is caught and swiftly punished, will refrain from following in his footsteps. There is little doubt that deterrence works much of the time: many ordinary citizens obey laws they might otherwise violate, simply out of fear of the consequences. (In times of civil riot, when sanctions are unenforceable, many of these same citizens take to looting local stores.) The effect of deterrent penalties on repeat offenders—people who have already been convicted at least once—or on those who painstakingly plan their crimes and assess the risks, is more problematical, however. That deterrence works much of the time is not in doubt; that it works with the terrorist population in particular is considerably less certain.

The third philosophy of corrections focuses specifically on the protection of society from the offender; the method is incapacitation, by which criminologists usually mean imprisonment rather than some of the modes favored in earlier times, such as execution or the chopping off of hands. Strictly speaking it would be desirable to incapacitate the offender only until he was no longer a threat to society. However, the impossibility of effectively determining when this point is reached has made most prison sentences a compromise between society's desire to see justice done and the recognition by courts and prison officials that there is very little likelihood that prison will improve offenders, and that meanwhile continued incarceration simply costs money and uses up a cell needed for someone else.

Finally, as an outgrowth of incapacitation and from a humanitarian impulse, we have evolved the concept and ideal of rehabilitation, which may mean altering the offender's outlook to conform with social norms, or facilitating his readjustment (economically, personally, socially) to life outside prison. The approaches to rehabilitation, and the theories of behavior modification behind them, have been numerous, the record of achievement mixed. Only a very few clear successes can be pointed to, and none of significance among incarcerated terrorists.

The ordinary offender sent off to prison is thus often fulfilling several social expectations at once. His lengthy incapacitation through imprisonment calms the fearful and may also serve as an effective deterrent. In addition it may satisfy society that retribution is being exacted through a punishment that fits the crime, while meanwhile the prison prepares the inmate, so it is hoped, for reentry into the world at large. Just as clearly, conflicts can arise when, either through successful efforts at rehabilitation or through more personal processes, an offender becomes ready to rejoin society not long after he has begun a lengthy prison term for a severe crime. He may be eligible for parole according to the letter of the law, and his parole board may agree that he should be released; yet feeling against him and his offense may run so high as to prevent the board from acting. Like other public institutions, the corrections system is essentially political and responsive to political pressures.

With such a diversity of expectations, such ill-defined possible outcomes, it is small wonder that the trial of a political terrorist is an ambiguous event. It presents problems of inherent bias, uncertain legal grounds for the trial, and complex motives whose relation to the case being tried is a subject of disagreement. In addition, media coverage may make the trial itself a continuation of the terrorists' effort to proselytize their cause.

To begin with the problem of bias: it is a truism among lawyers that in our time, when international law is still implemented through relatively primitive mechanisms, a political terrorist who has offended the interests of one or more countries will have a difficult time receiving impartial justice in a national court; yet there is no international court to which he can have recourse. Even if he is not obliged to be tried by a court of the country he has attacked, therefore, he will still face trial in a country subject to political pressures from allies and enemies. If he does not manage to escape trial by his own country, against which he has been battling, he may have little hope of sympathy or even fairness. At his trial in Athens in January 1973, Stathis Panagoulis testified, "I have been brutally tortured and kept under unspeakable conditions." To which Lieutenant Colonel Karamaios, chief judge of the military tribunal, replied, "What did you expect, the Athens Hilton?"

Clearly the questions discussed here are closely connected with those that arise when an apprehended terrorist faces extradition. Whether a given action is considered a political crime is of utmost importance to the alleged perpetrator, for it affects the legitimacy of his trial. However, the court will make this determination only after considering both his professed motive and the circumstances surrounding the case. These problems were nicely brought to the fore during the trial of the remnants of West Germany's Baader-Meinhof gang between 1975 and 1977.

At the beginning of the trial there were five defendants—Ulrike Meinhof, Andreas Baader, and three comrades. They argued that they were "prisoners of war" and "partisans" and thus their trial in West Germany on criminal charges arising from the murder of a German policeman and four American soldiers was irrelevant and illegal. They had some additional reasons for their claim. Evidence indicated the authorities had illegally bugged their prison cells, and the transcripts indicated the judge who heard their case was prejudiced. Had they been apprehended in another country it is possible that they could have successfully fought extradition to West Germany; as it was, convinced that their trial was a farce, they would have no part in it. Early in the proceedings one of the defendants, Holger Meins, went on a hunger strike and died a few months later. Meinhof, the ideological leader of the group, hanged herself (or was hanged, as her supporters charged) in a Stuttgart prison cell. Friends of the remaining three defendants hardly helped the chances of appeal by gunning down the chief federal prosecutor in the case, Siegfried Buback, along with a chauffeur and a bodyguard, at the trial's end.*

Biased or not, the court decided that in the army base bombings which killed the Americans, it was dealing not with a case of political action involving a conflict with the state of West Germany but with the common crime of murder. This decision was in line with what Bassiouni calls the "political-incidence" theory expounded in English law. The theory holds that a political crime (which would also be immune from extradition) must fulfill two conditions: it must occur during a political revolt or disturbance, and it must be a part of such a disturbance. As an English court stated the case in 1891: "The question really is, whether, upon the facts, it is clear that the man was acting as one of a number of persons engaged in acts of violence of a political character with a political object, and as part of the political movement and rising in which he was taking part." The problem is that in 1891 political terrorism was an undeveloped art; the crucial determination for a modern court is whether a political disturbance can be said to be taking place if only a tiny guerrilla band is engaged in committing murder for self-announced political ends.

* The story ended with appropriate ambiguity in October 1977 when, following the succesful West German commando raid on a Lufthansa jet hijacked by Baader-Meinhof sympathizers trying to spring their comrades, three leaders of the gang were found dead in their cells, one by hanging, two by gunshot. "Suicide," said the authorities, but they failed to explain the prisoners' access to guns in the face of rigid security measures.

The Baader-Meinhof gang believed they were engaged in a war with the West German capitalist state and that their actions against American soldiers were justified by America's illegal intervention in Vietnam. By their own definition there was a civil disturbance in the land. There was precedent, however, for the German court's skepticism. In an extradition case from the fifties involving a Chilean with the curious hybrid name of Guillermo Patricio Kelly, the defendant was a member of the far right rather than the far left, but the issues were similar. Kelly was charged with killing a gatekeeper during an attack on local Communist headquarters in Buenos Aires. He fled to his homeland and Argentina requested his extradition. In response he claimed the attack was political and he was therefore entitled to protection. The court found otherwise: "These crimes did not occur during an attack [by Kelly] on the security of the state, such as to be considered connected to a separate political offense. They took place at a time of public tranquility during which the murder and theft were isolated acts. The ultimate objective may have been the political one of annihilating communists, but the principles of public international law which this decision accepts do not admit that an ordinary crime is converted into a political one solely because of its ultimate objective."

The critical words here are "at a time of public tranquility." If the necessary condition of a political revolt or disturbance is that it involves the public at large, then most terrorist bands have little chance of achieving the favored status, since only at relatively late stages in their revolutionary programs can they hope to involve more than a few people in their small, intense wars. For the West German court, as for earlier courts with similar cases, a bomb at an American military base and the shooting of a policeman during a bank robbery staged to help fund gang activities did not constitute the general public disturbance that might have validated the group's claim to the status of political criminals, partisans, or prisoners of war.

Thus the legal grounds for the Baader-Meinhof trial were established by deciding that the motive of the defendants, however ardently political, was not in itself sufficient to grant them a status as political prisoners, and that the prosecution was right in its allegation that their crimes were merely cold-blooded murders. To the end the remaining defendants refused to appear in the courtroom, even to hear the reading of the verdict. At the conclusion of a two-year trial held under the tightest security regulations the court found the trio guilty of murder and imposed life sentences on all three.

In all such cases the national court trying professed terrorists faces a frustrating dilemma. It must respond to pressures from its own government and from an anxious populace to punish the offenders sternly, both in retaliation for their violent actions and to make an example of them. At the same time it cannot help being sensitive to international opinion which tends to sympathize with any move to protest repressive policies of an established government, provided such a move is not directed at one's own government. It is worth adding that by no means all countries subscribe to the theory of political crime outlined in the case of Guillermo Kelly, and that other standards have been erected which do not require a general uprising as the only setting for a certified political offense. Thus a court may have deep reservations about trying defendants for ordinary assault, murder, or expropriation of property when their motive was clearly political —and yet feel compelled to do so to maintain the national interest. All this argues for the establishment of an international court. Just how the sentences of such a court should be carried out is a problem not yet solved.

There is yet another reason why the trial of terrorists in national courts is a dangerous enterprise for the government concerned. Like the terrorist act itself, such a trial is a media event. Earlier we noted that the problem of pretrial publicity may adversely affect the interests of the accused offender once he comes before a judge and jury. But the other side of the coin is that the trial can energize and perpetuate the publicity that surrounded the initial terrorist activities. A good actor and manipulator can turn a courtroom into a theater in which to present his case to a wide audience vividly and with no little pathos. In America the past master of this technique was Bobby Seale, whose trial on charges of conspiracy to incite riot in connection with the 1968 Democratic Convention in Chicago summed up for his countrymen the implacable opposition between the nation's youth and minorities, who lacked formal power but were convinced they were right on the issues of personal freedom and opposition to an unjust war in Vietnam, and the "establishment," the white middle class anxious to preserve its values and perquisites and jealous of assaults on its character and dignity. Seale—not a true terrorist by any sensible definition—symbolized the former; his nemesis Judge Julius Hoffman symbolized the latter.

Admittedly the government had a thin case. Invoking an old law forbidding travel across state lines for the purpose of inciting to riot, government prosecutors claimed Seale, along with the group that came to be known as the Chicago Seven—Rennard Davis, David Dellinger, Tom Hayden, Abbie Hoffman, Jerry Rubin, John Froines, and Lee Weiner—had conspired to come to Chicago with the express intent of provoking some ten thousand protesters to engage in violent demonstrations and bloody battles with the Chicago police. In the first place, conspiracy is an extremely difficult crime to prove, since it requires the prosecution to be privy to conversations and plans held in advance of the event. Attempting to demonstrate such knowledge, the prosecution introduced tapes of phone conversations between some of the defendants, admitting that it had obtained them by wiretapping. On appeal, this evidence was ruled inadmissible. Second, the contention that anyone other than the Chicago police themselves had provoked the confrontation was virtually impossible to defend: clearly the demonstrating crowd had tried to get to the convention center and to the Conrad Hilton Hotel where many of the delegates were lodged, and clearly the police had tried to prevent them from doing so. The demonstrators were unarmed and obviously no match for the club-swinging cops. Along with reporters and photographers covering the scene, they were wounded in far greater numbers than the police.

Quite apart from these issues, which were played out in his courtroom, Judge Hoffman proved no match for Seale as a showman. As the trial proceeded before an audience packed with sympathizers of the defendants, Hoffman rose to every bait Seale laid for him. He blustered at every obscenity, every gesture. He repeatedly cited Seale and his lawyer, William Kunstler, for contempt of court. Finally, on Hoffman's orders, the court marshals dragged Seale from the courtroom and gagged him with a white muslin cloth. They brought him back in and shackled him to a gray steel folding chair with leg iron and handcuffs. In spite of the gag, spectators in the courtroom could hear him saying, "I want the right to speak on behalf of my constitutional rights." Hoffman heard him too, and was evidently dismayed, for he sent the marshals out with Seale for a second time, telling them, "I don't think you accomplished your purpose with that contrivance." When they returned after a recess they had plastered strips of white adhesive tape over the cloth gag in Seale's mouth. Temporarily mute, Seale proceeded to rattle his chains till Hoffman ordered they be replaced with leather straps. This was done, but Seale worked free of the straps, tore off the tape and gag, and shouted, "Let me cross-examine the witness! I still want to cross-examine the witness!"

The image of a young black man bound and gagged in a court presided over by an elderly white judge, a member of the power structure who clearly had neither comprehension of the issues nor sympathy for the defendant, stuck in Americans' minds and served as a rallying point not only for antiwar sentiment but for all antiestablishment feeling. It hardly mattered that the charges against Seale were eventually dropped. In this case far more was done for the cause of the Chicago Seven in Judge Hoffman's courtroom than could have been done if the defendants had simply been set free and forgotten. With hindsight, even given the chance, many liberals, and probably Bobby Seale himself, would not have changed a thing.

By their conduct during their trials, people charged with "terrorist" crimes reveal much about the real depth of their terrorism. Clearly the Baader-Meinhof people were far more alienated from the society sitting in judgment on them than Seale and his codefendants were from theirs. For the Baader-Meinhof defendants the trial was meaningless, a mockery. They did not acknowledge the laws that made it possible. It was not their game; they did not accept its rules. (Though their willingness to appeal their life sentences suggests either an uncharacteristic compromise with the methods of the establishment or a recognition that "playing the game" offered them a better chance of freedom, given the documentable errors of the case, than a spectacular but risky escape attempt.) On the other hand, it is clear that· for Seale and the Black Panthers, as for most of the white "radicals" being tried in Chicago in 1969, the basic premises on which the trial was supposed to operate were very important. Far from shunning the system, Seale used every opportunity to make it work for him. He requested that the trial be delayed because his lawyer was recovering from an operation. When that request was denied he attempted to represent himself. Whenever he could wrench his gag free it was to say something like "I want . . . to speak on behalf of my constitutional rights" or "I want to cross-examine that witness." Such statements presuppose commitment to a constitution and a legal system that functions by due process, and Seale never repudiated that commitment. Similarly, Eldridge Cleaver in 1968, while ostensibly preaching radical violence, carefully made it conditional on the failure of political process: "We need lawyers today who have a lawbook in one hand and a gun in the other . . . so that if [the lawyer] goes to court and that shit doesn't come out right, he can pull out his gun and start shooting." The Baader-Meinhof gang, like the Japanese United Red Army, were well past the point of giving the lawbook a chance; sneering at "juridical cretinism," they had already begun shooting.

If all the causes reviewed so far make the outcome of a terrorist trial problematical, so, in America, does the one institution sanctioned by tradition as the means par excellence of modifying an expected unfavorable outcome to a trial: that institution is plea bargaining. In its classic form plea bargaining involves pleading guilty to a lesser charge to avoid the aggravation of a trial on a greater one. As the sergeant investigating a burglary case put it when the time came to plea bargain with the suspect, "We know enough to make him feel that we got him by the balls. We have enough information so that we can almost tell him where he took a piss twenty-four hours a day for the last few days. Actually, we don't know what is what so far as real evidence is concerned, but we know so much about his general activities, that he thinks we know a lot more than we actually do."

In this way, if the defendant decides to bargain, the prosecution is saved the time and expense of proving the harder case; the defendant also saves time and expense but exchanges the possibility (usually very slim) of getting off scot-free for the certainty of serving a shorter sentence than he would have served if convicted on the heavier charge. When Susan Saxe was apprehended in Philadelphia five years after a Massachusetts bank robbery (with political overtones) in which patrolman Walter Schroeder died and in which she was implicated, her lawyers spent long hours preparing her case for trial. After the trial, which lasted twenty-seven days, the jury finally returned to announce it was hopelessly deadlocked. The trial was declared a mistrial. It would have to be conducted all over from scratch.

At this point Saxe thought soberly about her options. She might risk another trial, but she had put all she had into the first and had not been able to convince twelve carefully selected people that there was a reasonable doubt about her guilt. The next time all might well agree in finding her guilty as charged. Meanwhile, the prosecutor was disposed to bargain. He too had worked hard on the case, yet he had not been able to convince twelve people of Saxe's guilt. Moreover, the case was now six years old; there was no longer a public clamor that the defendant be found guilty of first-degree murder, though there would have been anger if she had gotten off with a not-guilty verdict. The prosecutor had better things to do, but he needed a conviction. So he suggested Saxe plead guilty to a manslaughter charge and accept a twelve-year sentence with credit for two years served while awaiting trial and a possibility of parole in six more years. It was a way out Saxe was looking for and she took it. She announced that she was pleading guilty to manslaughter not because she *was* guilty but to save herself further aggravation at the hands of the American judicial system. "I do not recognize the right of the state to a single day of my life, but I do recognize its power to take that and more. This guilty plea was a tactical decision based on that reality."

It is this cooling of public sentiment on which the terrorist's ability to plea bargain depends. If his trial takes place immediately after the terrorist action, then he will have little leverage in seeking lenient treatment from court and prosecutor. However, if through various strategies, including going underground as Saxe did, he can manage to delay the trial till the initial passions have died down, then the likelihood is that a deal can be struck. The public, which tends to change its attitudes as new social pressures and prejudices replace old ones, may come to see the terrorist less as a victimizer, more as a victim, just as it began to see Patty Hearst, by 1976, as a victim of SLA histrionics and coercion and her own privileged, empty upbringing. Or just as it began to see William Calley, leader of the American army squad that massacred over a hundred Vietnamese civilians at My Lai, as the victim of a standard war mentality, on the one hand, and the simplistic willingness of Americans to use him as a scapegoat, on the other. The solution in both cases, interestingly enough, was to confine the "convicts" under house arrest, allowing both the maximum freedom consistent with the American notion of just punishment. Hearst's "house arrest" was engineered and paid for by her father as a condition of keeping his daughter free on bail pending her appeals. Calley's, ordered by Richard Nixon, kept him under guard in an officer's apartment in Fort Benning, Georgia, until after many months of legal wrangling he was finally set free in October 1975, having served just a third of his ten-year sentence. America has not formally acknowledged the notion of the terrorist as political prisoner, but for Hearst and Calley, both of whom fit that description, legal mechanisms were bent to provide a very near approach.

It is an impromptu response to the vexed question: what do you sentence the terrorist *to*? And in the case of both Hearst and Calley the expectations were comfortingly similar, making the answer to the question easier than it often is. Both erstwhile terrorists wanted to be reassimilated. Their political convictions were minimal. They were in fact accidental terrorists—Hearst because she had been coopted into a revolutionary group she was too weak to resist, Calley because he had taken the daily bloodthirstiness of army life at face value, had asked no questions and shown no personal scruples, and had the misfortune to be "discovered" at a time when domestic revulsion to the war was nearing its height. Furthermore, for each prodigal a pattern of rehabilitation already existed in American life. The young person who goes out, falls in with bad companions, has a fling involving some lawbreaking and some sexual misbehavior, and returns to the nest sadder and wiser and ready to settle down is an oversimplified but real model that Patty's elders were familiar with and which they immediately applied to her. The soldier who gets used to killing and brutality in war, then comes home and learns, at least in theory, to forget all that and become a solid family man is a pattern that has been familiar to Americans for generations. They found it increasingly difficult to see the difference between Calley and the young veteran down the street—and perhaps they were right.

But not all terrorists fit these models; in fact, most do not. Most are ideologically sophisticated, committed consciously and for well-argued reasons to goals not accepted by the society that convicts them. If brought back into the mainstream and shown leniency, they are not likely to become prosperous insurance salesmen. What is to be done with them?

Of the functions of prison sentences enumerated earlier, three make some claim to changing the long-term behavior of offenders or potential offenders and might, therefore, be appropriate measures to use in order to reduce the incidence of terrorism. The prospect of a long sentence might deter prospective terrorists, or proper rehabilitative measures might reform those who are caught, or at the very least, the terrorist would be incapacitated—prevented from inflicting further harm—while in prison. So goes the theory, which lies behind the periodic United Nations attempts to adopt a convention calling for the punishment of terrorists by the signatory nations, and behind the attempts of countries like Israel and West Germany to secure the extradition of a terrorist like Daoud so that each might have the privilege of trying and sentencing him. But each of these reasons becomes problematical in the case of the terrorist.

In order for deterrence to be effective, the threat of imprisonment must work as a substitute conscience in the potential offender, making him weigh the costs of committing a crime against the benefits he might derive. How heavily the costs will count depends, of course, on the likelihood that the piper must actually be paid, as well as the anticipated severity. The ideologically convinced terrorist makes this calculation in a way that is disconcerting to law enforcement officials. He says, as in the Mau Mau oath, "I will from now onwards fight the real fight for the land and freedom of our country till we get it or till my last drop of blood." Or he says, as Karari Njama said, "There is no playing with either arrow or gun. Whenever you pull the trigger or release the arrow from the string, you cannot stop it by any means from hitting the object you aimed at. This means that we have started our fight for Land and Freedom; whether you like it or not, whether you surrender or not, our aim must at last be achieved by either you or your children." That is, the obstacles to any one person are insignificant; death or imprisonment count for very little (in theory) with the committed terrorist, since he is devoted to a goal in whose light these things are of no importance. Beyond this, terrorists in many parts of the world are aware of the extreme unlikelihood that they will actually be imprisoned. We shall look at figures in a moment.

Rehabilitation is, if anything, even less likely to succeed. Recidivism, the rate at which released prisoners are reconvicted, is high enough with all major crimes to cast doubt on the efficacy of prison rehabilitation programs, and, indeed, the available studies are far from providing clear evidence that rehabilitation efforts really work. In the case of terrorists such doubts are reinforced by the insistent question: what social or psychological maladjustments are being attacked by the rehabilitative effort? Is the terrorist out of adjustment or, as he would ask the question, is society out of adjustment? In a contest of ideologies it makes little sense to speak of either side as being reformed. Some judicial systems have recognized this. In the case of a British conscientious objector sentenced to the Borstal School for "rehabilitation" during World War II, the appeals court overturned the sentence, observing that reformation of prisoners did not extend to matters of conscience.

Tom Hadden, a Belfast jurist, maintains that some modest successes have been achieved in the Irish internment system in providing prison educational programs in social theory and Irish history for young terrorists, who may decide on the basis of such experiences to pursue their ideological goals by parliamentary means rather than by terrorism. But the available evidence offers no way of telling whether the "modest successes" are accounted for by rehabilitation or by normal attrition from the ranks of the combatants. Furthermore, there has really been no effective way to keep track of individual terrorists in Northern Ireland and make sure that today's new IRA recruit was not in the same army a year ago, before he did a stint as an interned terrorist undergoing "rehabilitation" through education.

Even if deterrence and rehabilitation are questionable concepts in dealing with terrorism, the law-and-order man argues that simple incapacitation through a long sentence is a gain because it protects society. What figures we have, however, tell a sad story to the contrary. It appears that, in most countries, including some with a reputation for severity, terrorists are not likely to go to jail in the first place, and that when they do they stay only a short while. Between 1968 and 1974 Israel apprehended 210 Arabs (and failed to apprehend at least that many more) on charges of political terrorism. By 1975 half of this number had gone free without a trial. Either sufficient evidence could not be collected on them, or it could not be collected in the time during which the accused terrorists were legally held. Beyond that figure an additional one fourth soon escaped or were released from prison in response to extortion attempts by outside terrorist groups. Finally, one fourth were sentenced, but nearly all were released before the end of their prison terms. In early 1976, of the original 210 prisoners apprehended, only three were still held inside Israeli jails. It seems unlikely that a would-be terrorist figuring such liberal odds would find in them much to deter him, and indeed there is no evidence that prison sentences in Israel or elsewhere, as presently meted out, offer the public any significant protection from terrorism.

For comparison purposes we can look at another population, the hijackers of U.S. aircraft. Since hijacking began as a serious business in the early sixties, the Federal Aviation Administration has kept a running tally, and at the beginning of 1976 it issued a report showing that of 244 hijackers, less than a third (79) had been convicted. Sixteen more (6 percent) had been killed during capture or had committed suicide. Of the convicted hijackers, only 54 were still in prison in 1974 when the practice of skyjacking in the United States effectively stopped. It's important to stress that not all those people were political terrorists; nevertheless the odds of being caught and imprisoned for a long term, though higher than for terrorists in Israel, did not reduce the rate of plane hijackings in the United States. What brought them to a virtual halt was not deterrence but "target hardening"—the introduction of airport security inspections in 1974.

Granted, however, that imprisoning the terrorist may offer some minimal protection to society, if only for a short period, it pays to look more closely at the nature of that protection, which varies depending on the "auspices" of incarceration. It is possible to establish special prisons for terrorists and other "political" offenders, but most courts in Western countries have sentenced terrorists to the same prisons inhabited by other people convicted of common crimes. Inside a typical prison, however, a terrorist is a strange and sometimes dangerous person. Prisoners tend to be from lower social and educational levels, because it is lawbreaking on these levels, frequently taking the form of violent depredations on persons and property, that most angers and frightens the middle class controlling the criminal justice system. Such prisoners are the losers of society—those who not only have turned to crime out of disaffection or need but have had the misfortune to get caught at it, usually more than once. They are often poorly educated and usually apolitical. Their hostility toward the system, while real, is disorganized and submerged, and it is the business of the prison guards to keep it that way. Placed in the midst of such a group, a terrorist can give political focus to suppressed anger and resentment. Usually better educated and more articulate, he can point out defects in the larger social structure that may be the source of the prisoners' difficulties with the law. He can add that by organizing and applying certain kinds of pressure to the power structure, a few people can force it to make major concessions. If he is successful in these efforts he can thus recruit several people to his cause and simultaneously create a prison atmosphere that may be beyond the capacity of the guards to handle.

The elements of organizational ability and political radicalism came together in California's Vacaville State Prison in the late 1960's when a group of black prisoners formed the Black Cultural Association, a self-help group devoted to educating its members and establishing communication with the outside world. The organization arose from a growing political consciousness among black prisoners, but it derived special impetus from two other sources. The first was Donald DeFreeze, a prisoner who was in and out of the institution, sometimes on probation, sometimes reincarcerated, and who had a fondness for guns and explosives. DeFreeze was energetic, charismatic. He was at Vacaville from 1969 until 1972 when he was transferred to Soledad Prison. There he escaped a few months later by simply walking away from a work detail, to be reunited with his former Vacaville comrades outside of prison, in Oakland. DeFreeze had the qualities of a leader but no particular direction in which to lead. That direction was supplied by the second element, an infusion of what Californians call "Berkeley radicalism" into Vacaville's Black Cultural Association. Initially begun by Colston Westbrook, a teaching assistant at the University of California at Berkeley, the BCA gradually established more contacts with the university and expanded its membership to include Joe Remiro, Russell Little, and Willie Wolfe. Wolfe was the only university person in this group; the other two were his roommates, also involved in radical politics. Their contacts with the BCA led to a further widening of the circle. Through talks at Peking Man House, a self-styled revolutionary commune near the Berkeley campus, Wolfe and his friends interested a number of young white women in the prisoners' group, and before long they were making visits to Vacaville, discussing politics with the prisoners, and having sex with them. Among these women were Patricia Soltysik ("Mizmoon"), Nancy Ling Perry, Angela Atwood, and Camilla Hall.

These two influences finally coincided in 1972 when De-Freeze rejoined his released comrades and quickly assumed leadership of a diverse group of black ex-cons and white radicals. A vignette is telling: DeFreeze, now going by the revolutionary name of Cinque, and calling himself a field marshal, cooking meals in Soltysik's apartment and writing down the revolutionary slogans and theorems she dictated. During this time he was laying plans for organized campaigns by the gradually cohering band that was starting to call itself the Symbionese Liberation Army.

The activities that resulted earned the group the label "terrorist," though the political focus of its campaign was always fuzzy and at times the rhetoric and violence exceeded any obvious political or social rationale. Given the composition of the SLA, however, this political naïveté is not at all surprising. It stemmed from student radicalism grafted onto the poisonous strength of black hostility, which had been cultivated over years of frustration with the polite racism of white society. The black prisoners were angry but had no program save violence. The white students were angry as well but had no program either, only rhetoric. The result of their anger was loud and deadly, but it still did not produce a program. Nevertheless, the subsequent slaying in Oakland and the kidnapping of Patty Hearst were sufficiently terrifying to Californians and the nation at large to serve as a warning of the dangers attendant on politicizing a prison population, or even a portion of it.

Not only can prison settings breed terrorist groups that later can wreak notable damage in the outside world, but politicized prisoners can also stir up trouble while still behind bars. Many have caused no little embarrassment to prison officials and society in general by using terrorist tactics to focus attention on corrupt or degrading conditions inside prison walls. The riots at Attica, so ineptly handled by police and Governor Nelson Rockefeller, were merely the most notorious in a series of uprisings in American prisons that recur periodically given the right combination of anger over grievances, inmate leadership, and provocation by guards.

They were also, in microcosm, an example of the way in which terrorism is bred by continued denial of access to power and exacerbated by violent, fearful reactions from those who hold that power. In September 1971 more than a thousand inmates of the New York State correctional facility at Attica rioted and seized thirty guards as hostages. Threatening to stab or club their captives to death, they issued over a makeshift megaphone a series of demands not very different from the recommendations reformers had been voicing for generations. The demands included coverage by the state's minimum-wage laws, the right to engage in political activity, real religious freedom, an end to prison censorship of reading material, the right to communicate, at their own expense, with anyone they chose, rehabilitation programs related to the realities of the outside world, better food, better health care, more recreation and less cell time, and no reprisals for the uprising. The response of prison authorities and Governor Rockefeller was to boggle at the inevitable demand for amnesty while agreeing to the other points. Apparently in the heat of the moment and the chagrin of the experience the illogic of the situation escaped them: they agreed that the demands were just and tacitly conceded that it had taken a major riot to bring the problem to public attention and wrest a humane solution from those in charge; yet they insisted on the necessity of punishing the prisoners—mostly black and Puerto Rican—for using what were clearly the only means at hand to force a solution to all but unbearable grievances. Their position hardened when one hostage died of injuries sustained during the first day of the revolt. In response the prisoners escalated their demands. The situation stalemated; then the intervention of sympathizers from the outside, including senators, representatives, and Black Panther head Bobby Seale, brought the two sides once again within talking distance, and the more unrealistic demands (such as the one for transportation of the perpetrators to a "non-imperialist" country) were dropped. Still the authorities refused to budge on the issue of complete amnesty, and the prisoners would accept nothing less.

Then, three days after the riot began, on Rockefeller's orders a thousand state troopers, sheriff's deputies, and prison guards stormed the prison under a heavy cloud of tear gas and blasted the prisoners with rifles and shotguns. As the bullets rained around them the convicts, who had gotten to know the hostages better during the crisis than in years of prison living, refrained from cutting their throats as they had threatened to do. "I don't have the heart to kill you," one told his captive. Nevertheless, nine were killed, and autopsies showed all had died of gunshot wounds. The prisoners had no guns.

Besides the hostages, thirty inmates were dead. Two others had been killed by their fellow convicts before the attack.

The aftermath was predictable. Prison authorities announced that the "efficient, affirmative police action" had been carried out with "extreme reluctance," and the governor's office blamed the uprising and its conclusion on the "revolutionary tactics of militants." Indeed they were, but they need not have had such a bitter end; they might have been better listened to.

As a result of this and similar episodes of hostage taking

in other prisons, police and guards have learned of necessity the basic psychological and strategic tools for managing the prison hostage-taking episode and bringing it to a successful conclusion. Even more than a hijacking or other hostage-taking enterprise on the outside, a prison uprising using terrorist techniques is a desperate undertaking, for it occurs in a known location surrounded by guards and police with good communications and by a frightened and often hostile community. Though they stand to lose the lives of hostages if they act rashly, prison officials still have a great deal of control, including access to the prison and food, light, and heat for the prisoners. Time, in short, is on their side and they can afford to play a waiting game. Doing so not only saves the lives of the guards who have been held hostage, it also saves the lives of prisoners and prevents a huge swing in public sympathy toward the prisoners and their grievances that inevitably occurs if some of them are killed. This control is a mixed blessing, however, since the conditions in most prisons beg for change and the lot of most prisoners is poor enough that it can do little to improve either their self-concept or their disposition to society; yet such improvements are the foundations of successful rehabilitation.

For these reasons prison officials may prefer to isolate convicted terrorists in a separate prison, or at any rate a separate cell block, to prevent their "contaminating" ordinary prisoners with revolutionary ideas and tactics. Such a move would require, in the first place, that courts or the prisons themselves distinguish between offenders who are terrorists and all other offenders, a distinction that Western courts have been reluctant to make, as already observed. They fear that acknowledging a political motive as a distinctive basis for prosecution or punishment would lead to prosecutions *merely* on grounds of politics. The law has yet to explore sufficiently the possibility of defining the offense of political terrorism as one that entails two separate elements, both of which must be present: a common crime and an announced political purpose behind that crime. If this were done, at least there might be a rational basis for separating convicted terrorists from other prisoners.

But would such segregation be advisable? Prisons are run by a tyranny of the few over the many: the guards over the inmates. Guards exercise their dominion by bullying prisoners through force or the threat of force and by working systematically to keep prisoners' self-esteem at a low ebb. Through formal and informal discipline, taunts, withholding of privileges, and arbitrary changes of day-to-day rules and procedures, guards manage to make prisoners feel stupid, incompetent, and worth very little in the social order. Guards do this because they are frightened; they are in charge of men who have committed violent crimes and may have incentive to commit others, and they are forcing such men to live in a way that is very unpleasant for most of them. They are doing this because it is their job, but they know it is a good way to get hurt. Consequently they use the most obvious means at their command to "keep the men in line." These means rely in large part on basic traits that a good many prisoners bring with them to prison. On the outside, few offenders occupied positions of responsibility and power. Most came from lower social strata whose members had relatively less to say than their middle-class neighbors about the course their lives would take. Their lives in prison, therefore, are in large measure a continuation of these power relationships, with certain exaggerations designed to make life easier and safer for the guards. It is hardly necessary to add that such conditions do not often prepare people for responsibilities and self-discipline in the outside world, which is the ostensible aim of rehabilitation programs.

But modes of prison discipline that rely on low self-images among the inmate population are ill suited to a collection of imprisoned terrorists. Such people do not as a rule come from the lowest levels of society but are, by contrast, among the better educated, even though they may belong to ethnic groups that have experienced unjust treatment. As individuals they are not used to being powerless, but are experienced at leading others and ingenious at finding ways to assert their wills. They therefore present a major discipline problem for guards who are used to coping with a more tractable population. In Northern Ireland, authorities originally experimented with camp-type prisons to accommodate the large numbers of people being arrested under an internment law which allowed for detention on suspicion of terrorist activity alone, not just on conviction. However, the prisoners quickly organized themselves into paramilitary groups and exerted strong pressure to conform on other prisoners who were less than completely committed to the implacable terrorism of the true Northern Irish partisan. To reduce the number of terrorists who could be in communication in such a prison system, authorities began transferring prisoners from camp-style prisons to those organized in cell-block style. But such a transition takes time, and even then the effectiveness of the cell-block system is debatable. From separate cells and even separate prisons the members of the Baader-Meinhof gang kept in touch by means of messages smuggled out by their lawyers. So effective was their communication system that when one of their number still at large gave evidence to the police, copies of the police report on his testimony soon made their way to the imprisoned gang members. A few days later the young man was found dead in a Berlin park with a bullet in his head. Prison did nothing to hurt the gang's discipline.

In the late sixties and early seventies California experimented with certain cell blocks devoted to groups of political dissidents. However, these prisoners also quickly organized themselves into paramilitary groups. Violence erupted, and several prisoners and guards were killed. Lawrence Bennett of the California Department of Corrections concluded in a 1975 study: "A significant portion of the violence [in California prisons is] related to quasi-political organizations that have many of the characteristics of the underworld gang." He might better have said, "of an elite army." For these reasons, coupled with the heightened danger of escapes by prisoners using the terrorist tactics that landed them in prison in the first place, it is likely that the large-scale segregation of political terrorists in prison would create as many problems as it would solve.

If imprisonment of terrorists in the manner of ordinary criminals is a solution that leaves much to be desired, there is still the model of the prisoner of war, which, because of the terrorist's attitude toward the government he pits himself against, may seem the most appropriate model after all. It is important to know what we mean by "prisoner of war," however. If we wish to emulate actual wartime practice in recent times (as opposed to the earlier practice of simply killing enemy troops rather than capturing them), there are several consequences it is important to take into account. First of all, a prisoner of war, like any other prisoner, is subject to the vagaries of treatment in whatever country incarcerates him. France, as we have seen, accords such prisoners a special treatment as provided by statute. They are required to perform no work and to wear no uniform. They may engage in more correspondence than ordinary prisoners and have more visitors. Political prisoners are accorded the same rights. In the Soviet Union, by contrast, a political offender or prisoner of war is considered guilty of maintaining ideas opposed to the people's welfare. The aim of internment for such persons is not only to incapacitate but to correct. Political prisoners are, therefore, subjected to a mixture of hard work and political indoctrination.

Second, a prisoner of war remains a prisoner only until the war has ended and an agreement is made between the countries involved for the exchange of prisoners. But a political prisoner such as a terrorist is often not engaged in a war that will be concluded in his lifetime. Unless one subscribes to the Russian idea of rehabilitating political prisoners by indoctrination, therefore, the terrorist treated like a prisoner of war is in effect sentenced to an indeterminate prison term, which can amount to a life sentence. Such a sentence may appeal to those who believe only the severest measures can curb the threat of anarchy and violence, but it takes insufficient account of both the prisoner's and the general society's ability to change. Eldridge Cleaver returned to the United States from exile in Algeria in 1976 emotionally committed to a system he had derided and violently attacked eight years before. American society, in the meantime, had grown notably less uncomfortable with the militance Cleaver represented, and more willing to assist black people in furthering their goals. The United States was still far from an easy society for a black person, but it was a possible society, and Cleaver now perceived it as such.

Third, if political prisoners are given a special and in some ways favored status by comparison with ordinary criminals, society is faced with the problem of deciding who rates such treatment. In the case of the terrorist the problem is especially difficult, not only because terrorism contains elements of both political and common crime but because, as we've repeatedly discovered, the balance between the two elements shifts from one terrorist group and foray to another. A kidnapping or bombing may look, or be contrived to look, very much like a terrorist exploit, whereas in reality it is nothing more than a device for extorting money or wreaking revenge. If these cases should come to the courts for decision, what guidelines do we expect judges to apply? This question has not yet been adequately dealt with, since in few courts in the world is the option available of sentencing the terrorist to serve time as a political prisoner. But even in the United States, which disavows the notion of political prisoners, unofficial arrangements have been made, as noted earlier, in the Hearst and Calley cases to mute the effects of confinement. It could be argued, however, that this was done out of deference not to the political consciences of the defendants but quite pointedly to the lack of such consciences: to the minor role played by conscious thought and decision in their crimes. Had Hearst and Calley not been other people's dupes (in this case the SLA's and the American Army's, respectively), but instead ideologues who planned and executed their own campaigns against cherished American institutions, it is hard to imagine courts showing a similar leniency—or society approving if they did.

What alternatives remain? One can confine the terrorist for a time and then keep him under surveillance upon release. But this is expensive and only moderately effective. Police and security organizations keep lists of dangerous characters whom they keep an eye on during major public events or when a dignitary makes an appearance, but constant surveillance of someone once convicted of terrorist activities would have little to recommend it and would produce serious questions concerning the civil liberties of the ex-offender population. Another alternative, decriminalization, carries some of the same problems as the practice of treating terrorists like prisoners of war: the question to be decided is, which offenders are sufficiently genuine terrorists to justify the extraordinary treatment? Beyond that, most people remain convinced that even if terrorists are not deterred *enough* by prison sentences, they are deterred *somewhat*. Few decision makers would be willing to give carte blanche to all terrorist acts, with no criminal penalties attached, for fear of allowing their country to become the terrorist capital of the world, with both an internal and an international trade fed by dozens of terrorists seeking refuge every month from prosecution for violent activities conducted elsewhere. Yet a large number of countries are unwilling to say unequivocally that terrorism should be stopped.

The disconcerting fact is that those countries wishing to eliminate terrorism from the world—and they do not appear to be in a majority—are forced to content themselves with halfway measures. Either the standard punishments do not impress terrorists dedicated to making sacrifices for the sake of an ideology, or they call forth a violent response from those still able to fight—one more battle in the continuing war between the entrenched establishment and its sworn enemies. Security measures, though they can be enhanced, can never be impermeable to determined terrorist incursions.

Meanwhile terrorism flourishes. Conditions are right when a group in power feels so threatened by those beneath it that it tries to scare them into submission, or when a group denied access to power concludes that the only way to achieve self-determination is to seize the reins by force. In either case exploitation is a key cause, and the contention that exploitation is rife in this century throughout much of the world is not only a staple of Third World political rhetoric, it is also true. Terrorism is a common resort because no one, in or out of power, abhors violence enough to renounce it. The popularity of terrorism has been growing because it works—not all the time, but often enough. In the gamble of human affairs, it is a relatively good bet. Those concerned to reduce the violence of terrorism have to reckon first with the subtler violence of legitimate power. In the sweep of history those systems of government that make power available impartially to all parties are extremely rare. The means are still being invented, and invention does not come as easy as destruction.

EPILOGUE

ONE OF THE BASIC POINTS MADE IN THE PRECEDING CHAPTERS —that *terrorism works*—has not been lost on terrorists, nor on those countries that stand to benefit from terrorist activities. If the terrorist enterprise worked in one place, they reasoned, organized by a few would-be revolutionaries to further a cause lacking the strength of either arms or numbers, it should work elsewhere, better financed, better organized, better armed. Just as the mercenary soldier appeared wherever there were battles to be fought and armies willing to hire him, so the terrorist-on-contract is making his appearance in our own day. In theory at least, the mercenary was a man without an ideology —one who would fight for any side that paid his price. In romance he was a man in love with adventure, and with some private integrity above the lines of battle.

In the United Red Army terrorists of Japan and in the activities of some South American groups we have examples of contract terrorists who, by contrast, adhere to an ideology that apparently transcends any particular political manifestation. The specific issues at stake in a given country are unimportant; the power relationships or the historical background weighs very little. What is said to matter is the destruction of *the capacity to exploit*, wherever it may be found—and if this effort entails the destruction of government altogether, then so be it. In general the capacity to exploit is equated with capitalism, and capitalism, whether or not tempered by democracy, is equated with fascism. "We are not fighting solely because of frustration with the profit-seeking theory," explained a member of Sekigunha, the society behind the United Red Army. "What we will never accept in this world is the fact, brought about by capitalism, of people exploiting other people. And *this* is our motive for being willing to fight, and being prepared to use all possible means in our fight."

As readily as in traditional warfare, brutal means are put forward to accomplish what seem humanitarian ends, and the theorist touts the necessity that other people should die for the sake of his own mild-sounding principles. The similarity is more than coincidental. We may, in fact, be witnessing a replacement of the means, if not the ideologies, of traditional warfare by the techniques of international terrorism. Burgeoning populations have driven many nations into a peculiar and unprecedented dilemma: as the competition for territory grows more acute, the historically normal means of resolving conflict have become, for related reasons, too expensive. To settle the struggles into which modern population growth has catapulted us, modern warfare is increasingly helpless: for it takes huge resources of energy and material to fuel even a single one of the world's great armies, and such resources are no longer available on the scale required. Brian Jenkins of the RAND Corporation observes, "No nation or insurgent group can afford to mobilize all its resources to fight for two generations. Protracted wars must compete with peacetime demands for resources. To fight long, one must fight cheaply; to fight cheaply, one must accept long periods of military stalemate." Under such circumstances it is clear that terrorism has something to offer a world so strapped for resources and yet so viciously at odds with itself that it must make a little violence go a long way. This is the terrorist's specialty—and what better way to use it than through leagues between the small nations bent on maintaining or aggrandizing their territory and the organizations whose special skill is in the application of maximum leverage through strategically chosen violent acts?

Amid the diverse and conflicting nationalist interests that have sponsored terrorist enterprises, it is possible to discern some similar ideologies: the concern that economic and social opportunity be equally available to everyone; the hatred of "exploitation," by which the theorists among these groups appear to mean the use of anyone's existence, talents, or labor for ends which he has not freely sanctioned; the desire to minimize the sway of government over individuals. That terrorism as a mode flies in the face of all these ideologies is not more disturbing to its adherents than the idea of a vicious and protracted war to "make the world safe for democracy" was to an earlier generation. If there is a common "language," then, among the world's major terrorist groups, it centers on a violent and implacable hostility to exploitation—of poor people by rich people and rich governments, and of weak nations by strong. Though exploitation is not clearly defined, it is such a language that makes it possible for the IRA to talk with the Palestine partisans, or for the Baader-Meinhof leaders to talk with a well-connected terrorist from Venezuela. They do more than talk, for, of course, in this business the most effective words are bullets.

Disclosures in the mid-seventies confirmed what dispassionate observers had long known without proof; that the two dominant ideologies of the world had employed, and would likely continue to employ, all means, fair and foul, to confound their enemies and gain, or retain, supremacy. The capitalist ideology is not commonly championed by small groups of the dispossessed, but it can employ such groups in the service of aims determined by large capitalist nations. So the United States trained Cuban exiles for the Bay of Pigs invasion of Communist Cuba and in effect molded what might have been an indifferently successful terrorist group into an embarrassingly unsuccessful army. Not content with that enterprise, the government expended no little ingenuity trying to concoct a plot for killing Castro—including a box of poisoned cigars. In this case the dispossessed were passed over in favor of a more businesslike and familiar ally, the Mafia. Yet even a contract with this ordinarily reliable eliminator of domestic undesirables (from the Mafia's point of view) failed to bring off the naïvely desired assassination.

It can happen that a Communist nation will employ the services of terrorists for a parallel end, but commonly terrorist groups do not need the instigation of a "contract" from a major government. They are committed enough in their own right to the ideal of world revolution to bring about international socialism that they need little prodding to make connections with each other around the globe, to provide technical assistance, logistical and military support. The network is large and loose; the terrorist organizations in it are in general willing to assist in the overthrow of any government, on the ground that most governments have been corrupted by power and that any replacements will almost inevitably lean farther to the left than their predecessors.

On such an understanding the Baader-Meinhof gang sent members to help the Palestinian hijackers on the expedition that ended up in Entebbe, and earlier, apparently after a personal visit from the leader of the Popular Front for the Liberation of Palestine, George Habbash, the United Red Army sent a trio of gunmen to handle an important job at Lod airport. The contract work continues. Most terrorist organizations will accept help anywhere they can get it. Members of the Irish Republican Army have received training from Arab guerrillas, and the organization has been partially financed through contributions of Irish-Americans, who in all likelihood did not know how their "relief" money was being used, and partially armed by American gunrunners, who knew very well what they were doing when they bought up supplies of pistols and automatic weapons in New Hampshire and sent them streaming back to the old sod.

An international conspiracy of terrorists in the sense of a tightly knit central directorate with tentacles around the globe, instant communications, a large budget, and implicitly obeyed orders is a figment of fearful imaginations, but clearly terrorists are as able as anyone else to make use of rapid transportation, telecommunications, and the anonymity of large cities to forge links, networks, and agreements. A keen insight into the nature of these connections came to the French government in July 1975 when undercover agents in Paris discovered that three diplomats attached to the Cuban embassy had been spending large amounts of time in an apartment with some notoriety. It was not a sex scandal. The apartment was rented by one Ilich Ramirez Sanchez, a rather pudgy young man who, under the nom de guerre "Carlos," may be the world's most famous terrorist. The middle son of an eccentric Venezuelan radical who named his children successively Vladimir, Ilich, and Lenin, Carlos had been educated at Moscow's Patrice Lumumba University, where he was presumably trained in the basic arts of terrorism. He proved an apt pupil. He had masterminded the kidnapping of OPEC ministers in Vienna in December 1975, and had successfully dodged numerous attempts to capture or kill him. At one point an informer led two police officers to Carlos' apartment. They rang the bell.

"Have to ask you to come down to headquarters for questioning. If you're who we think you are, there may be a warrant out for your arrest. . . . Yeah, you can go to the bathroom first, but don't be all day." Carlos came out of the bathroom with automatic weapons blazing. All three of his visitors fell to the ground. As the terrorist moved past them out the door he paused to pump another bullet into the head of the informer, who was still writhing on the floor. Then he stepped outside and faded into the anonymous night life of Paris.

Now France's Direction de la Surveillance du Territoire, a counterintelligence group, had information that Carlos was affiliated with the Popular Front for the Liberation of Palestine. The PFLP confirmed, since, after all, such news could only contribute to its image, that there was indeed a connection. It was known further that Carlos had never shed his ties with certain South American terrorist groups, who were now forming a "junta for revolutionary coordination" binding guerrilla units from Chile, Argentina, Bolivia, and Uruguay, and in fact two Venezuelan women—compatriots of his— were also expelled from France because they were in close contact with the Cubans. Finally, it was possible to document linkages between Carlos and the Japanese United Red Army, on the one hand, and the Baader-Meinhof gang in West Germany on the other. By frequenting Carlos' Paris hideout, therefore, the Cubans were showing far too great an interest on the part of their country in fomenting socialist, or at least anticapitalist, revolution on an international scale. Such revolution is, of course, one of the tenets of Communism, but it did not sit well with France, European independent though she might style herself. The authorities still couldn't manage to capture Carlos, but they could serve Cuba with a warning on the subject of terrorism—and they chose this lesser course.

The elusive terrorist had the last laugh, however. In an ironic gesture he sent letters to the French counterintelligence group and to Scotland Yard naming six undercover agents who worked for the American CIA and Israeli intelligence services. Then he vanished and was next reported seen in London's Chelsea district by a woman who had known him years earlier.

So we have seen Latin American terrorism linked to Palestinian terrorism; we have seen Arabs giving technical assistance to the Irish Republican Army; and we have seen the IRA fraternizing with the Basque separatists in Spain. We have seen the United Red Army sending a suicide squad to perform a massacre for the Palestinians; we have seen Germany's Baader-Meinhof gang lending support to these other groups; and we have seen all of them appearing and disappearing in Europe, Latin America, and the Middle East, going about their business with a certain amount of discreet support from established governments.* Some of these groups have purposes distinctly related to a concept of national identity: the Palestinians are intent on regaining a homeland for their displaced people, and the more militant of them are intent on pushing Israel into the sea. The IRA intend to free themselves from England and from Protestant dominance. Neither group has the overthrow of capitalism as a main tenet of its ideology; yet that tenet is what links the interests of the groups that come to their aid and secures the desultory support of Communist nations. Terrorism is a plausible weapon of the dispossessed, and to the dispossessed any social system that can be portrayed as exploitative is odious.

Terrorism is also the plaything of those who imagine what it must be like to be dispossessed. The students and former

---

* At the center of this network reputedly lurks Wadi Haddad, a Palestinian who, according to Israeli intelligence sources, numbers Carlos and the Japanese URA terrorists among his deadly employees.

students who fed the meager ranks of the SLA, Baader-Mein-hof, and the United Red Army had not known hunger, nor did they face a lifetime of exclusion from the ranks of power. They had no need to fight for land or a national identity. But the distance between their experience and their imaginations tended only to make them more promiscuously dangerous. Neither their anger nor their methods were well focused. They took to social protest the way some people take to crime. It filled a need for adventure; it expressed passion and diffuse anger; it gave them instant power and notoriety that they could justify in terms of very general but important-sounding ideals like "people's revolution" and "anti-imperialism." It also made them, in effect, hired guns. Easy as it was for them to convince themselves that their hijacking and murders were supporting important causes in various parts of the world, they became the servants of those rarer groups locked in genuine struggles in which there were high personal stakes. It is extremely doubtful that Carlos had any clear plan or goal for social change, and it has become embarrassingly clear that the Baader-Meinhof people did not. They were at the beck and call of anyone with a suitably "anti-imperialist" cause, in much the same way as the Mafia had been, on occasion, for hire by the CIA. The difference is that the Mafia had cost a lot more and, on the available evidence, was less effective.

"Contract terrorism" is not attractive, and it does little to inspire faith in either the probity or the morality of the partisans who expound its pseudorevolutionary rhetoric, but compared with the havoc of outright, full-scale warfare it may well be the lesser of two evils. Attempting in 1975 to prognosticate future trends, Brian Jenkins speculated, "Low-level violence may increase and become more troublesome while conventional wars become fewer and shorter. The overall number of casualties may decline. Indeed, a future world of many Ulsters could turn out to be far less violent in total casualties than the past sixty years during which approximately 23 million soldiers and between 26 and 34 million civilians died in two major wars. When it comes to slaughter, the 'civilized' nations of the world can do it on a far greater scale than those we now call 'terrorists.' " The point is well taken. Residents of Belfast like to point out that the homicide rate in that city, taking into account all terrorist bombings, knifings, and shootings, is still substantially below the homicide rate in Detroit.

The fear of terrorism and its future evolution is based on a projection of the tendencies of conventional warfare onto the quite different mode of guerrilla warfare—but such projections may be based on false assumptions. Nations depending on traditional military organizations, whose purpose in the final analysis is to kill, rate their security in terms of their ability to kill the maximum number of enemies or potential enemies—soldiers and civilians alike. If the ability to destroy the earth's population ten times over is, paradoxically, a measure of security, it is easy to see why such nations would expect the terrorist, in his pursuit of power, to desire similar destructive potency—in a word the possession of nuclear weapons with which he might, at the very least, blackmail any nation on earth. It is the stuff nightmares are made of. It might happen; but it is probably not the highest priority of most terrorists, and for the good reason that they have become past masters at the art of blackmail with far lesser means. The ingenious discovery of the terrorist is that the strategic rather than the massive application of force suffices to bring a nation to its knees. If the threatened death of a few dozen people will effect a reorientation of power, to what purpose is the actual death of a few million? It would be useful, from the terrorist's point of view, to terrorize a whole city. It would be excellent to be more than a match in firepower for any police force that might try to disarm you; but a nuclear capacity is hardly necessary for such purposes. Unless, of course, a police department also boasted a nuclear "deterrent," in which case the citizen's safest course would be to evacuate the city. A nuclear police force and a nuclear terrorist organization are about equally unnerving in prospect.

What really lies behind the popular fear of extremely powerful terrorist organizations is very primitive: it is fear of the new, the strange, the sudden and unwanted change in status brought on by a different social order. Even in those countries born of revolution, most people are fearful of further revolution. For all its inequities the present social order is fairly comfortable to most citizens of the powerful, technologically advanced nations—East and West. In their complex hierarchies of power the man in the street cherishes his place. If some people profit now and then by his discomfort, he at least profits by that of his less well placed neighbors. And if there is abject misery in the system of things, it is not too visible; its claims and accusations are not too strident. But terrorism—or any mode of revolution with an outside chance of success—threatens to upset all this. It threatens to strip away old prerogatives, take hard-won possessions by force, substitute a new and as yet ill-defined ethic for whatever we have now, and, worst of all, place some loud lower-class ideologue in the seat of power. It offers, in short, a distinctly unattractive future.

What is needed to retain perspective in all this is a kind of double vision. "See," said the tottering King Lear, "how yond justice rails upon yond simple thief. Hark in thine ear: change places and, handy-dandy, which is the justice, which is the thief?" It is not too much to imagine a future in which the currently wealthy nations, having exhausted their resources of energy and raw materials, pursue their lost power as avidly as such power is now sought by the Third World. It is not too hard to imagine them having recourse to the by-now traditional weapons and tactics of the militant weak and the dispossessed. Under such conditions hostage taking, surprise attacks against the innocent, the destruction of property, and the relentless iteration of demands would be the most natural methods, defended by elaborate theory, of the very people who now organize "management conferences" to cope with the nagging terrorist threat worrying their heels. We need not deceive ourselves: we know the techniques and have already found them useful, on past occasions, ourselves. When the time comes when they are perceived to be necessary, our politicians will have ready justifications for their use. We are the terrorists of tomorrow.

NOTES

Books and articles are cited in full on first appearance and thereafter by the author's last name or a short title. Quotations not cited in these notes can generally be found in major newspapers with the dateline mentioned in the text.

TEXT
PAGE

13   Leila Khaled said this in October 1970 and is quoted in *Time,* November 2, 1970.

13   Carlos Marighella's *Minimanual of the Urban Guerrilla,* the source of the quotation from him, is printed in Jay Mallin, ed., *Terror and Urban Guerrillas: A Study of Tactics and Documents* (Coral Gables, Fla., 1971), pp. 70 ff.

13   The remarks of the United Red Army terrorist, as well as various other pronouncements of terrorists quoted in this book, were recorded by Gerald McKnight in *The Mind of the Terrorist* (London, 1974). These are in the chapter "Bushido Spirit," p. 168.

18   The FLN author of this observation was Abane Ramdane, quoted in Roland Gaucher, *The Terrorists* (London, 1968) and in Anthony Burton, *Urban Terrorism* (New York, 1976), pp. 135–36.

19   Shevlin to McKnight in *The Mind of the Terrorist,* p. 74.

28   Guevara's theories are well discussed by Walter Laqueur in *Guerrilla* (Boston, 1976).

31   Marighella, quoted in Mallin, pp. 72–73.

32   Njama's autobiography of his life in the Mau Mau is contained in Donald L. Barnett and Karari Njama, *Mau Mau from Within* (New York and London, 1966), pp. 434–35.

32   Paul Wilkinson, *Political Terrorism* (London, 1974), p. 46.

32–33 Marighella, quoted in Mallin, p. 71.

35   Prosser's "Some Questions on Tactics" is excerpted in Mallin, p. 60 ff.

TEXT
PAGE

36 Viet Cong directive on "Repression," printed in Mallin, p. 31 ff.

36–37 Karari Njama in *Mau Mau from Within,* p. 373.

38 Prosser, "Some Questions on Tactics," in Mallin, pp. 62–63.

39 O'Bradaigh to McKnight in *The Mind of the Terrorist,* p. 57.

39 Marighella, quoted in Mallin, p. 103.

43–45 Quotations and the general outline of this account are from Daniel Lang, "A Reporter at Large (Swedish Hostages)," *The New Yorker,* November 25, 1974, p. 56.

45–46 Lorraine Berzins' experience is described by Linda Laushway in "Trust—The Key to Hostage Incidents," *Liaison* (Ottawa, Ministry of the Solicitor General), February 1976.

47 Flannery O'Connor, "A Good Man Is Hard to Find," in the collection of stories *A Good Man Is Hard to Find* (New York, 1955).

50 ff. Wolfgang Salewski, *Luftpiraterie* (Munich, 1976). The skyjacking attempt narrated in the following pages is based loosely on the Lufthansa training film, though it also draws on other episodes. The interpolated comments of the crew members were recorded by Salewski in interviews with flight crews who had been hijacked. The translations are mine.

59 An excellent encapsulation of the events leading up to the Chinese revolution in 1949 is contained in the introduction to John Melby's *The Mandate of Heaven* (Toronto, 1968).

61 Sharif to McKnight in *The Mind of the Terrorist,* p. 24.

68 Figures cited are those of the Federal Aviation Administration.

71 For a treatment of the psychology of airplane hijacking, though with very little attention to political terrorism, see David G. Hubbard, *The Skyjacker: His Flights of Fantasy* (New York, 1971).

73–74 Karl Markus Kreis, "Terrorism Remains a Global Problem," translated from *Europa Archiv* 11, 1976, and printed in *The German Tribune* 28, October 1976.

75–76 Maire Drumm to McKnight in *The Mind of the Terrorist,* pp. 52–53. Italics are in the original.

TEXT
PAGE

77   Melby tells the story of Chiang's capture in *The Mandate of Heaven,* introduction.

84   Yehezkel Dror, "T.F.B. (Terrorism, Fanaticism, Blackmail) as a Strategic Problem," a position paper prepared for a symposium on Terrorism, Pre-emption, and Surprise, Hebrew University, Jerusalem, June 1975.

91   Stanley Milgram, *Obedience to Authority: An Experimental View* (New York, 1974).

95   At the Santa Margherita (Italy) Management Training Seminar on Hostage Taking, May 13–15, 1976, sponsored by the International Centre for Comparative Criminology, University of Montreal, the terms "primary" and "secondary" victims were introduced by Ronald Crelinsten in a working paper presented to the conference.

97   Conor Cruise O'Brien, "Reflections on Terrorism," *The New York Review of Books,* September 16, 1976, p. 44.

98   Brian M. Jenkins, "International Terrorism: A New Mode of Conflict," paper prepared for the California Seminar on Arms Control and Foreign Policy, December 1974.

98   Fayez A. Sayegh, "The Palestine Problem and the Role of the P.L.O.," mimeographed pamphlet available through the Arab Information Center, New York, N.Y.

100   Bolz is quoted by Barbara Gelb in "A Cool-Headed Cop Who Saves Hostages," *New York Times Magazine,* April 17, 1977, p. 87.

104   The Ehnmark-Palme dialogue is reproduced by Daniel Lang in the *New Yorker* article cited earlier.

104–5   Bolz in Gelb, "A Cool-Headed Cop."

115–16   The ambivalence of the American press over the Vietnam War is documented by Phillip Knightley in *The First Casualty* (New York, 1975).

117   Barbara Gelb quotes the psychiatrist in "A Cool-Headed Cop."

128   McKnight, p. 102.

129   Romeo to McKnight in *The Mind of the Terrorist,* p. 100.

130–31   The use of terrorism in the Algerian revolution is analyzed by David Fromkin in "The Strategy of Terrorism," *Foreign Affairs,* July 1975, p. 683.

133–34   Njama in *Mau Mau from Within,* pp. 401 ff.

139   Knightley, p. 236.

140   Knightley on Berlin, p. 311; quoting Murrow, p. 313.

140–41 Knightley on Dresden, p. 313.

142   Harvey's fighter-bomber pilot is quoted in Knightley, p. 385.

142–43 Knightley on racism, p. 386.

143   Ché Guevara, "Message to the Tricontinental" in *Ché Guevara* (Havana, 1968).

144   Knightley, p. 394.

145   United Red Army terrorist to McKnight, *The Mind of the Terrorist,* p. 165.

149–50 Jacob W. F. Sundberg, "Thinking the Unthinkable or the Case of Dr. Tsironis," in M. Cherif Bassiouni, ed., *International Terrorism and Political Crimes* (Springfield, Ill., 1975).

152   Edward Legge, *King Edward in His True Colors* (London, 1912), pp. 81–82.

152–53 The Guatemalan decision is cited by Bassiouni in "The Political Offense Exception in Extradition Law and Practice," in his volume *International Terrorism,* p. 398.

153   The definition is given in ibid., p. 408.

154   The Yugoslav decision is cited by Theo Vogler in "Perspectives on Extradition and Terrorism," in Bassiouni, p. 394.

154   The Palestine case (8 *Palestine Law Reports* (1941), p. 43) is cited by Bassiouni in "The Political Offense Exception," *International Terrorism,* p. 409 n.

154–55 The *actus reus* and *mens rea* quotation is from Bassiouni, ibid.

157–58 M. Léauté's ideas were presented at the Basic Issues Seminar on the Impact of Terrorism and Skyjacking on the Operations of the Criminal Justice System, Rochester, Michigan, February 5–7, 1976, and will be found in the proceedings of that seminar published in 1976 by the International Centre for Comparative Criminology, University of Montreal.

162–63 These recommendations are presented in "Final Document: Conclusions and Recommendations," in Bassiouni, pp. xix and xx.

166   Figures on terrorism involving U.S. businesses are cited in *Counterforce* magazine, January 1977.

169   Seale to McKnight, *The Mind of the Terrorist,* p. 142.

174   For a discussion of prison rehabilitation and whether it works, see Douglas Lipton, Robert Martinson, and

TEXT
PAGE
───

Judith Wilks, *The Effectiveness of Correctional Treatment: A Survey of Treatment Evaluation Studies* (New York, 1975).

175 The Greek exchange is quoted by Amnesty International in *Report on Torture* (London, 1973), p. 95.

176 The English court ruling (1 *Q.B.*, 149 (1891)) is quoted by Bassiouni in "The Political Offense Exception," p. 398.

177 The Chilean court hearing Argentina's extradition request is quoted by Bassiouni in "The Political Offense Exception," p. 415.

182 The sergeant is quoted by Jerome Skolnick in *Justice without Trial* (New York, 1966), p. 177.

185 Njama in *Mau Mau from Within,* pp. 131, 185.

186 In addition to the Lipton study cited earlier, further literature on rehabilitation and recidivism is reviewed by John Hudson in *The Evaluation of Patuxent Institution* (1977), chapter 3, available from Contract Research Corporation, Belmont, Mass.

186–87 Figures on prison retention rates among Arab terrorists are from Bart DeSchutter of the University of Brussels, and are included in the Michigan seminar proceedings cited earlier, published by the International Centre for Comparative Criminology, University of Montreal. Figures on U.S. hijackers are supplied by the Federal Aviation Administration.

194 Bennett's study is called "Prison Violence in California: Issues and Alternatives" (1975) and is available from the California Department of Finance, Sacramento.

199–200 United Red Army terrorist to McKnight, *The Mind of the Terrorist,* p. 167.

200 The quotation from Brian Jenkins is taken from the paper "International Terrorism: A New Mode of Conflict."

205 Brian Jenkins, ibid.

INDEX

African anticolonialists, 28. *See also* Mau Mau
AID (U.S. Agency for International Development), 21
Airport security, 29; adoption of systems for, 89, 90; effect on rate of skyjackings, 67, 68; impact on passenger freedom, 68, 69; symbolic value of, 67, 68
Albania, 149
Alexander of Serbia, 152
Al Fatah, 78
Algeria, 98, 130, 131, 157, 196; position on hostage taking, 164
Algerian nationalists, 130-32
Algiers, 18, 130, 131
Allende, Salvador, 94
American Foreign Service Association, 89
American Revolutionary Army, 23
Amin, Idi, 86, 159
Amman, 124
Anarchism, contrasted with terrorism, 97
Anticommunism, U.S. policy of, 145
Anti-imperialism, 13, 205
Arafat, Yasir, 25
Argentina, 159, 177, 203; and ERP, 21, 22
Assassination, 16, 32; and extradition, 152; attempts on Fidel Castro, 201; attempts on U.S. presidents, 63; psychological impact of, 66
Assassins (Muslim sect), 32
Asylum, political, 148; and Abu Daoud, 157; and extradition treaties, 150-53 *passim*; law concerning, 154
Athens, 79, 175
Atlanta, 23
Attentat clause, 152
Attica, 26, 100, 190
Atwood, Angela, 189

Baader, Andreas, 175
Baader-Meinhof group (Red Army Faction), 49, 97, 116, 128, 156, 205; trial of members, 175-78, 181

Baena Alonso, José Francisco, 171
Bank of Montreal, 47
Barcelona, 171
Basque separatists, 28, 98, 171-72; connections with IRA, 204
Bassiouni, M. Cherif, 153, 176
Bay of Pigs, 201
Beirut, Israeli raid on, 79
Belfast, 75, 131, 186, 206
Belgium, 124, 151, 152
Bennett, Lawrence, 194
Berkeley, 115, 188, 189
Berlin, 194; World War II bombing ordered by Churchill, 140
Berzins, Lorraine, 45-48
Beyer, Fritz, 152
Biological warfare, 73
Black Cultural Association, 189
Black Muslims, 105
Black Panthers, 169, 181, 191; and Chicago shootout, 81-83
Black Politics, 35
Black Power, 28, 161
Black September group, 119, 123
Bolivia, 128, 203
Bolz, Frank, 100, 104
Bombing: incidents of, 14, 15, 17, 35, 130, 176-77; psychology of, 37-39
Bonn, 156
Borstal School, 186
Böse, 49, 50
Brazil, 13, 14, 31
Britain: air war during World War II, 139; presence in Northern Ireland, 75, 76; terrorist acts in Palestine, 81; vote in U.N. on Israeli censure, 79
Buback, Siegfried, 176
Buenos Aires, 22, 177
Busic, Zvonko, 45, 61

California, 22, 98, 189; and isolation of political dissidents in prisons, 194; Vacaville State Prison, 189
Calley, William, Jr., 143, 183, 184, 196
Calzadilla, John, 23
Cambodia, 159

Canada, 29, 45, 129, 148; invokes War Measures Act, 19; kidnapping of James Cross, 108
Canadian Penitentiary Service, 45
Capitalism: as a terrorist target, 49, 98, 132, 145, 176, 199; goals served by terrorism, 201
Carbonneau, Marc, 110
Carey, Richard, 87, 104
Carlos (Ilich Ramirez Sanchez), 74, 202; links with terrorist groups, 203-6 *passim*
Carter, Jimmy, 106
Castro, Fidel, attempted assassination of, 201
Central African Republic, 165
Charles de Gaulle Airport, 34, 87, 112
Chemical warfare, 73
Chiang Kai-shek, 59, 77
Chicago, 33, 35, 86, 129; battle between Panthers and police, 81-82; Democratic National Convention (1968), 178-79
Chicago Seven, 179, 180
Chile, 94, 177, 203
China, 77
Chinese Communist Revolution, 26, 77
Chinese Nationalists, 77
Chou En-lai, 77
Churchill, Sir Winston, 140
CIA, 204, 205
Civil rights, 197; conflict with terrorism, 27, 36, 37; impact of increased security measures on, 72. *See also* Freedom, personal; Human rights
Clark, Mark, 82
Cleaver, Eldridge, 181, 196
Colombia, 79, 118
Committee on Extraordinary Dangers, 89
Communism, 145, 204
Communist nations, 204
Concessions, as a negotiating tool, 100, 110-11, 120-21, 123
Contract terrorism, 198, 201, 202, 204, 205
Costa-Gavras, Constantin, 21, 22
Crime, common: contrasted with political crime, 20, 98, 127-28, 153-55, 162; in international law, 150, 153-55, 162
Crime, political: contrasted with common crime, 15, 16, 20, 23, 24, 154, 155; defined, 152, 153, 176, 197; history of concept, 150-51
Croatian nationalists, 33-35, 45, 61,
74, 86, 93, 98, 104, 112, 116, 131
Cross, James: kidnapped in Quebec, 108, 109; released, 110; role of media in kidnapping of, 114
Crusaders, 32
Cuba, 110, 146, 166, 201, 203, 204
Cuban exiles, 146, 166, 201
Cullinane, Maurice, 106, 107
Czech nationalists, 28

Daoud, Abu, 124, 155-62, 185
David, Yitzhak, 49-50
DeFreeze, Donald (Cinque), 188, 189
Democratic National Convention (1968), 129, 178
Detroit, 206
Diplomats and diplomacy, 14, 20, 87, 88, 124, 138
Direction de la Surveillance du Territoire, 203
Displacement, defined, 92
Dog Day Afternoon, 122-23
Douglas, Tommy, 19
Dourrah, Youssef Said Abu, 154
Dowding, Sir Hugh, 139
Dresden, 137, 140
Dror, Yehezkel, 84
Drumm, Maire, 75-76
Dulles International Airport, 69-70
Dutch government, 118

Eban, Abba, 86
Echeverría, Angel Otaegui, 171
Echo effect, defined, 21
Eckerman, Richard, 152
Edward VII, 152
Egypt, 150, 156
Ehnmark, Kristin, 43, 104
Eichmann, Adolf, 159
Eid, Guy, 124
Electronic detection devices, 67-70 *passim*, 166. *See also* X-ray detection devices
Ellsberg, Daniel, 153
Entebbe, 49, 84, 86, 114, 117, 119, 124
ERP (Ejército Revolucionario Popular), 21, 22
ETA. *See* Basque separatists
Executive Protection Service, 62
Exploitation, 199, 200, 201, 294
Extradition, 27, 156-60; and attentat clauses, 152; legal principles concerning, 162, 163; treaties, 122, 148, 150, 151, 152, 157, 166

FBI, 115, 161

Federal Aviation Administration, 68
Fiat Motor Co., 21
Fields, Marshall H., 63
Fighters for a Free Croatia, 33-35
FLN (Front de Liberation Nationale), 18
FLQ (Front de Liberation du Québec), 29, 108, 109, 129
Ford Motor Co., 22
Fort Benning, 183
France, 34, 130, 131, 152, 204; ancient extradition treaty, 150; pursuit of Carlos, 202-3; treatment of Abu Daoud, 155-58, 160; treatment of convicted terrorists, 157, 158
Franco, Francisco, 26, 28, 171, 172
Freedom, personal: impact of security measures on, 19, 64, 68, 69, 72, 128
Freedom of Information Act, 115
French-Canadian separatists, 28, 29. *See also* FLQ
French Revolution, 27
Fromkin, David, 131

Game theory, 95, 96
García, Ramón, 171
Geijer, Lennart, 43
Geneva, 172
Geneva Conventions, 79
Gennaro, Giuseppi di, 80
Germany, 139, 140, 152. *See also* West Germany
Ghorbal, Ashraf, 106-7
Gilmore, Gary, 91-92
Giscard d'Estaing, Valéry, 156, 157
Godfrey, David, 47
Grand Central Terminal, 35
Greece, 26, 148-49, 154
Grotius, Hugo, 150
Guatemala, 152
Guevara, Ernesto (Ché), 26, 28, 128, 143

Habbash, George, 202
Haddad, Wadi, 204n.
Hadden, Tom, 186
Hall, Richard, 121
Hampton, Fred, 82
Hanafi Muslims, 63, 105-6, 132
Hanrahan, Edward V., 82-83
Harvey, Frank, 142
Hattusilis III, 150
Havana, 110, 146
Hearst, Patricia, 99, 117, 183-84, 190; kidnap of, 22; relationship to captors, 46, 48; role of media

in kidnap, 114, 115; sentencing of, 196
Hearst, Randolph, 22
Hearst, Mrs. Randolph, 115
Hijacking, 15, 24, 33-34, 49, 50, 58, 59, 68, 104, 146, 148, 187. *See also* Skyjacking
Hiroshima, 137, 141
Hitler, Adolf, 25
Hoaxes, terrorist: at airports, 69; by Croatian nationalists, 34, 112; nuclear, 73
Hoffman, Julius, 179, 180
Hostage taking, 24, 41, 65, 99, 117; contrasted with other terrorist acts, 94; responses to, 85, 87, 100, 101, 120
Hostages: as negotiators, 103-4; psychology of, 43-58 *passim*, 60, 90, 117-18; role in terrorist acts, 24, 117; Stockholm syndrome, 43-45
Hulsman, Louk, 170
Human rights, 151, 153

Interpol, 74
IRA (Irish Republican Army), 26, 38, 75, 98, 137, 186, 201, 202, 204
Iraq, 165
Ireland. *See* Northern Ireland
Islamic Center, 106
Israel, 27, 40, 41, 77, 78, 119, 137, 138, 145, 159, 160, 185-87, 204; condemnation by U.N., 81; Entebbe incident, 49, 84, 85, 114; Lod Airport massacre, 15, 16, 145; Ma'alot, 40, 87, 101, 125, 137; role in Daoud incident, 156-59
Israeli athletes, 15, 119, 155, 159
Israeli commandos, 78, 117, 159
Italy, 21, 69, 70, 80

Japan, 77
Jenkins, Brian, 98, 200, 205
Jerusalem, 78
Johnson, Lyndon, 130
Jordan, 78, 79, 124

Karamaios, Lt. Col., 175
Kelly, Guillermo Patricio, 178
Kennedy, John, 66
Kennedy, Robert, 66
Kenya, 36, 59, 98, 133
Khaalis, Hamaas Abdul, 105-8, 146
Khaled, Leila, 13
Khartoum, 124
Kidnapping, 13, 59, 60, 118; psychology of, 41-43

King, Martin Luther, Jr., 66
Kiritsis, Anthony, 121-22
Kiryat Shmona, 40
Knightley, Phillip, 139, 140, 141, 142, 144
KPFA, 22, 115
Kollek, Teddy, 78
Konkret, 129
Kreis, Karl Marcus, 73
Kunstler, William, 180

LaGuardia Airport, 17
Lanctot, Jacques, 110
Lang, Daniel, 43, 45
LaPorte, Pierre, 109, 110
Law: and political crime, 150-51; and terrorism, 24, 27, 148-50, 157; international, 27, 29, 124, 125, 146-47, 153-54, 164-66
Léauté, Jacques, 157, 168
Lebanon, 40, 79
Le Monde, comment on Daoud incident, 157
Letelier, Orlando, 94
Letter bombs, 16, 93
Leupin, Eric, 118
Lévesque, René, 29
Libya, 164, 165
Little, Russell, 189
Ljungberg, Lennart, 44, 45
Lod International Airport, 15, 16, 145
London, 33, 131, 140, 204
Long Island, 23
Lorenz, Peter, 116
Los Angeles, 101
Luftpiraterie (Air Piracy), 50
Lundblad, Birgitta, 44

Ma'alot, 40, 87, 101, 125, 137
Macomber, William, 124
Madrid, 171
Mafia, 201, 205
Mali, 165
Manotas, Juan Paredes, 171
Mao Tse-tung, 26, 36, 59, 77
Marighella, Carlos, 13, 31, 32, 39
Mark, Sir Robert, 100
Marshall, George C., 77
Mau Mau, 26, 32, 36, 59, 98, 133, 185
Mayaguez, 159
McKnight, Gerald, 19, 75, 128, 169
Media: effects of, 114-16, 175, 178; importance of, 61, 80, 98; role of, 16, 18, 22, 23, 35, 41, 42, 112-14
Meinhof, Ulrike, 175, 176
Meins, Holger, 176
Metropolitan Police (London), 100

Mexico, 67
Middle East. *See* Israel; Palestinians; PDFLP; PFLP; PLO
Milgram, Stanley, 91, 92
Minimanual of the Urban Guerrilla, 31
Mitrione, Daniel, 21, 113, 129
Moffitt, Michael, 94
Moffitt, Ronnie, 94
Mogadishu, 87n.
Mohammed, Messenger of God, 106
Molina, Edgar R., 22
Monson, Ronald, 141
Montreal, 33, 46, 108, 109, 110, 112
Moore, Cory C., 106
Moore, George, 124
Moscow, 40, 203
Munich, 50, 86, 119, 125, 155, 158
Murphy, J. Reginald, 23
My Lai, 116, 143-45, 183

Nagasaki, 137
Nahariya, 40
Nammer, Kamal, 78
Napoleon III, 151
Nazi Germany, 81
Negotiation, 29, 85, 95, 99, 100, 110, 120-22, 123; elements of, 105, 108; problems of, 87; refusal of, 65, 83-89, 100, 120, 124; successful, 119, 125
Negotiators, 47, 99-105 *passim*
New Hampshire, 202
Newspapers. *See* Media
New Year's Gang, 15
New York City, 33, 112, 136; police department, 100
New York Times, 27, 62, 97, 157
New Yorker, 45
Nixon, Richard, 183
Njama, Karari, 32, 36, 133, 134, 185
Noel, Cleo, 123, 124
Northern Ireland, 29, 40, 75, 76, 131; prisons in, 186, 194
North Vietnam, 142. *See also* Vietnam
Nuclear terrorism, 72, 73, 137, 206

Oakland, 22, 189
O'Bradaigh, Ruairi, 39
O'Brien, Conor Cruise, 97
O'Connor, Flannery, 47
Oldgren, Elizabeth, 44
Olofsson, Clark, 43
Olsson, Jan-Erik, 43, 44, 48, 49, 104
OPEC, 203
Ottawa, 129

Pakistan, 63

Palestinians, 13, 15, 28, 40, 41, 98, 138, 155, 156, 158, 159, 201, 202, 204; guerrillas, 123, 124, 130, 137, 201, 202
Palme, Olof, 43, 104
Papadopoulos, George, 148, 149
Papandreou, Andreas, 148
Paraguay, 79
Paris, 33, 34, 35, 45, 74, 86, 87, 112, 116, 130, 155, 202, 203
Patrice Lumumba University, 203
PDFLP (Popular Democratic Front for the Liberation of Palestine), 40
Peking, 71
Peking Man House, 189
People in Need program, 23
People's Army (China), 59
Perkins, Jim, 34
Perry, Nancy Ling, 189
PFLP (Popular Front for the Liberation of Palestine), 15, 40, 41, 202, 203
Philadelphia, 182
Phillips, John Aristotle, 73
Pilots, airline, 89, 104
Plea bargaining, 172, 181, 182, 183
PLO (Palestine Liberation Organization), 40, 41, 98, 135-37, 138; and Abu Daoud, 155, 156; training IRA guerrillas, 137
Plutonium, 72-73
Political incidence theory, 176
Political prisoners, 183, 195
Political refugees, 148, 150
Press. *See* Media
Preston, Robert K., 62
Prison reform, 24, 190, 193
Prisoner exchange, 104
Prisoner release, through terrorist activity, 14, 21, 101, 104, 108, 110, 116, 118, 124. *See also* Prisoner exchange
Prisoners of war, 27, 158, 175, 195
Prosser, George, 35, 38
Publicity: in relation to terrorism, 17, 22, 26, 98, 108, 112, 113, 131, 138; effects of on trial and sentence, 114, 175, 178

Quebec, 29, 108

Racism, 142, 143
Radio. *See* Media
RAF, 139
Ramses II, 150
RAND Corporation, 96, 98, 200
Ransom, 21, 23, 100, 118
Rappaport, 81
Remiro, Joe, 189

Revolution, 20, 30, 33, 35, 36, 133-35, 150, 151, 201-4, 207
Revolutionary Armed Forces, 118-19
Rheault, Robert, 144
Rhodesia, 29, 135, 165
Rockefeller, Nelson, 101, 190, 191
Rome, 69
Romeo, 129
Rosenberg, Julius and Ethel, 168
Royal Canadian Mounted Police, 109
Rush, Kenneth, 87
Russia. *See* Soviet Union

Sabotage, 35, 66, 110
Saffran, Louis, 62
Safstrom, Sven, 44
Saleh, Mahmoud, 155
Salewski, Wolfgang, 50
Sallustro, Oberdan, 21
San Francisco, 65
San Francisco Examiner, 115
Sanchez, Ilich Ramirez. *See* Carlos
Sanchez Bravo, José Luis, 171
Santa Margherita, 96
Sartre, Jean-Paul, 143
Saudi Arabia, 124, 156
Saxe, Susan, 182, 183
Sayegh, Fayez A., 98
Schroeder, Walter, 182
Scotland Yard, 204
Seale, Bobby, 149, 169, 179-81, 191
Security, 29, 62-65, 68, 88; economics of, 19, 67; impact on personal freedom, 19, 64, 68-69, 72, 128; limitations of, 65-67, 74-75, 197. *See also* Airport security
Seguin, Pierre, 110
Sekigunha, 199
Selten, Reinhard, 96, 97, 111
Sentencing, 183, 195, 196
Shamir, 40
Sharif, Bassam Abu, 61
Shevlin, Myles, 19
Sirhan Sirhan, 124
Skyjacking, 15, 24, 58, 59, 137; rate, 68, 166; deterrents, 187
SLA (Symbionese Liberation Army), 22, 23, 48, 98, 99, 101n., 114, 115, 117, 183, 189, 205
Smith, Ian, 165
Smith, Samuel, 92
Soledad Prison, 188
Soltysik, Patricia (Mizmoon), 189
Somalia, 86n., 164
South Africa, 29, 165
South American guerrillas, 28, 129, 199, 203
Soviet Unicn, 153, 168, 195

Spain, 29, 98, 171, 204
Stalin, Joseph, 66
State of Siege, 21, 22
Stockholm, 43, 45, 149
Stockholm syndrome, 43, 44, 45
Strategic Weapon and Tactics (SWAT) squads, 101
Stuttgart, 176
Sudan, 124
Sundberg, Jacob, 148, 149, 150
Sweden, 43, 148, 149, 150, 154
Switzerland, 154
Syria, 79, 153

Tanzania, 165
Target hardening, 62-93 passim; limitations of, 91, 92; effectiveness of, 186
Tel Aviv, 15, 85, 114
Television. See Media
Terrorism: against business, 166; as protest, 13, 199-205; causes, 27, 28, 169, 172; defined, 14-20, 35, 36, 132, 135, 167; future of, 200, 205-7; motivations for, 13, 14, 20, 24, 25, 32, 33, 98, 154, 155, 168, 169, 175, 192, 204-5; psychology of, 31-61; relationship to revolution, 20, 33, 36, 98, 128-35
Terzi, Zehdi Labib, 136-38
Third World, 79, 146, 164-66, 207
Tokyo, 68
Torture, 21, 91, 92, 148, 149, 175
Trotsky, Leon, 67
Trudeau, Pierre, 108, 109, 129
Tsironis, Vassilios, 148, 149, 150, 162
Tupamaros, 14, 21, 23, 113, 114, 129
Turkey, 15

Uganda, 49, 84, 85, 119, 159
Ulster Defence League, 76
United Arab Emirates, 164
United Nations, 13, 65, 81, 89, 137, 146, 164-66, 167; General Assembly, 136, 164, 165; Security Council, 78, 79
United Red Army (Japan), 13, 132, 145, 181, 199, 202, 203, 204-5
United States, 24, 34, 41, 63, 66, 69, 71, 73, 81-83, 106, 124, 130, 145, 156-57, 159, 166, 187, 195-96, 201; airport security techniques in, 67-68; policy on terrorism, 79, 83, 88, 89, 118, 124

University of California (Berkeley), 188, 189
Urban guerrillas, 14, 31, 134
Uruguay, 14, 21, 129, 203
Utah, 91

Vacaville State Prison, 189
Vance, Cyrus, 106
Venezuela, 201, 203
Victims: as intermediary, 19, 39, 40; primary, 95, 132; secondary, 33, 34, 37-39, 43-45, 95, 99, 104-5, 117-18, 119, 122-23, 132
Vienna, 203
Viet Cong, 36, 98
Vietnam, 66, 98, 144, 183
Vietnam War, 35, 36, 38, 66, 98, 115, 129, 142-44. See also My Lai; Calley, William, Jr.
Violence, 39-40, 91, 92, 129, 144, 198; against minorities, 169; against noncombatants, 137, 139-40, 142
Vorster, John, 28, 165

War, 29, 75, 83, 137, 200; contrasted with terrorism, 92, 139-44, 200, 205, 207
War Measures Act, 19, 109, 129
Warkworth Institution, 45
Washington, D.C., 62, 63, 70, 94, 105, 146
Westbrook, Colston, 189
West Germany, 15, 27, 49, 50, 96, 97, 185, 203, 204; and Baader-Meinhof group, 128, 129; in Abu Daoud case, 156, 157, 160; policies, 86, 89, 155
White House, 62, 63
Wilkinson, Paul, 32
Williams, Maurice, 106
Winters, Spurgeon, 81
Wolfe, Willie, 189
World War II, 77, 81, 139-43, 159

X-ray detection devices: effect on skyjacking rates, 166; use in airports, 67-69

Yaqub-Khan, Sahabzada, 63, 107
Yenan, 77
Yugoslavia, 34, 35, 154, 165

Zahedi, Ardeshir, 107
Zambia, 165